ACROSS AMERICA
with the boys

Matthew Collins

Published by:
MATC Publishing Ltd.
P.O. Box 11507
London
W14 9FX
United Kingdom

© Matthew Collins 1998

Published and Distributed by MATC Publishing Ltd. 1998
Reprinted 1999

Other titles:
Matthew's Travels 10 Years of Trips for 'The Travel Show'

ISBN   0 9528553 2 1

The extract on page 178 is from *Fear and Loathing in Las Vegas* by Hunter S. Thompson. Copyright © 1971 by Hunter S. Thompson. Reprinted by kind permission of HarperCollins Publishers, London and Random House, Inc., New York City.

Cartoons by Roğ

Cover design theme by Publicity Projects

Cover Photographs by Matthew Collins with help from Julia Bley, America Sanchez and Charles Ireland

Printed and Bound by MPG Books Ltd, Bodmin, Cornwall

To Charlie, Nicolai and my dad Patrick.

1 Cruise America, Orlando

The boys were charging around the motorhome showroom like two demented imps. I was trying to tie up the final paperwork.

'You say you're gonna be eleven weeks travelling alone with those two?' asked the incredulous receptionist. She was a friendly but blunt-talking woman.

'Yup.'

'Well, I take my hat off to you sir...'

'Thanks.'

'Just you and those small boys? All across America? For *eleven weeks*, you say? And no one to help you at all?'

'Nope.'

'Well, you are some brave guy... There aren't many men like you around today... No sir! I mean I can't imagine any man I know taking his kids away for a *weekend*, never mind for nearly three months. Yes sir, you are some brave guy...'

'Thanks.'

'So... We got you down for five thousand five hundred miles, dropping the motorhome on the nineteenth of August in Los Angeles...'

'Yup.'

'That's a pretty big trip... Which way you goin'? North first, then west? Boy, you know I almost envy you... Although I'm not sure *I'd* be comfortable, taking two small kids on my own. But you obviously know what you are doing and I think it's great. But are you sure you'll have *no* help on your trip?'

'Well... I will have some help.'

'Your wife's coming over to join you?'

'Well, she's coming over to *visit*. But an au pair girl will be coming over to *help* me.'

'An au pair girl?'

'Yeh, you know – like a nanny. A foreign student. A German girl. A nineteen-year-old. And then she's going back to Germany and a

5

Spanish girl's arriving.'

'Oh! I see! You're *not* stupid, are you? And there's me thinking you were going to be all alone like some poor motorhome househusband kind o' thing.'

'Well, I am going to be a *sort* of motorhome househusband. I mean I'll be with them twenty-four hours a day – and with no help at all for the first part of the trip. And au pairs aren't substitute parents. I mean, they'll just help out with daily tasks and things.'

'I understand... Your wife know about this? The arrangement with the German and Spanish girls and stuff?'

'Yes, of course she does. She helped me arrange everything.'

'Helped you *arrange* everything? Well, that's obviously a unique wife you got. Are all British women so understanding?'

'Actually, my wife's Russian.'

'Russian? Well, I don't know much about Russian women. But I guess they're pretty unique too... OK... If you could just sign here... You're taking the VIP Plus insurance, right?'

'Right.'

'Well, there you go, sir. Have a fabulous trip. Look after your boys. And those au pair girls.' And as a technician led us off to our newly rented motorhome the Cruise America receptionist winked at me.

The RV looked gargantuan. It was twenty-seven feet long, almost eight feet wide and just over twelve feet high. And I was the world's worst driver. At thirty-six I had never owned a car. I'd rented the odd hatchback, but this was a very different beast.

The technician pointed out features. 'OK... You got your electrical hook-up here, sewer there, water here, gas filler there.' Then we stepped inside. 'Fridge/freezer here, stove there, bathroom here, main bedroom there, dinette here (table by day – bed at night), overhead bunk up there. That's about it. Anything else you need to know?'

'Er... Are they easy to drive?'

'No problem, man! Same as a car. Just watch your height. Make sure you got enough clearance – twelve-foot-six minimum. And never reverse without someone guiding you.'

'And what about controls? Indicators and stuff...' (I was delaying the moment of departure.)

'Same as a regular Ford. Indicators here, handbrake there, lights just over here.'

'So you don't need any special driving skills?'

'Not at all. Have a good trip.' And with that he went. Leaving me to a six-and-a-half litre, V-8 powered motorhome with two children of three and four to guide me.

I pulled out slowly and swirled on to a frightening four-lane highway. I could hardly drive a small car. How would I handle this monster?

I came to some lights and braked. Cupboards flew open, crockery hit the floor and Charlie said: 'For goodness' sake, daddy!'

'Sorry, Charlie.'

'That's all right, daddy. Just try to drive more carefully.'

2 The Plan

Friends had questioned the wisdom of my plan. Now, with plates and cups sliding along the RV floor, I began to question it myself.

But when my sons were born my mum gave me some excellent advice: 'Enjoy your children.' That's what I was *going* to do. And they were going to have a fabulous time too.

The plan to cross America had been partly selfish. But I had wanted my boys to have the most fantastic summer. Charlie, the older one, was starting school that September so he would not have so much free time again for years.

The idea took shape after my wife, Khelga, started working. She is Russian and after five years in Britain had found her first job. She'd settled as a graduate, thinking herself a gift to the Western World. Then she found her qualifications weren't recognised by the Western World. She had a baby. Then another baby. And when she restarted job-seeking she found that attitudes still hadn't changed. So she acquired computing skills at evening classes to add to the five languages she spoke. Finally she had interviews and took a job in the City — with the Eastern European division of a big investment bank.

I continued working from home. I'd made a living writing and talking about travel but after becoming a dad had started to dislike frequent travelling (rather a professional handicap). I'd spent Charlie's first year travelling non-stop. I earned good money but hardly saw my son. Eighteen months later Khelga found her job. At twenty-nine she was hungry to progress. (And I was happy to encourage her — she's very bright and I'd always known that she would do well.) Khelga began work and was soon out of the house eleven hours a day. We hired an au pair girl and put both kids in a nursery. During the week, we hardly saw them.

Suddenly one morning, fed up with handing my children over to others, I had a simple idea. I would take a break, go away with the boys and give them twenty-four-hours-a-day attention. We would spend the summer in America. An au pair would help us. Khelga would visit but meanwhile could concentrate a hundred per cent (and guilt-free) on her new career.

'How are you going to pay for it?' she quizzed. 'And what about the mortgage?'

'I'll write a book,' I said. 'I'll publish it myself.' So I approached the bank with a business plan.

Luckily, my bank manager, David Woolley, was sympathetic. I'd already published one book (*Matthew's Travels – 10 Years of Trips for 'The Travel Show'*).

'Nice idea,' said Mr Woolley. 'But *will* it work?' I persuaded him it would and, to my amazement, he agreed a loan. So I bought the air tickets and hired the RV.

Tell people you're going away with your children for three months, while your wife stays behind to work and you'll get one of three reactions:

1 They'll say you're nuts
2 They'll say you're a hero
3 They'll say you're a swine – for leaving your wife behind.

Tell men you're going to be joined on your trip by an au pair and you'll get only one – the obvious – reaction. Why is it that whenever you mention foreign au pair girls, a cliché of randy husbands chasing nubile blondes comes to so many blokes' minds? Few male friends could believe Khelga was happy to let me travel with two au pairs.

The first would be Julia from Cologne. She already worked for us and would fly over from London after finishing her English course. Julia was practical, intelligent, extremely well organised and fantastic with the children. I liked and respected her enormously. But the idea of complications with this efficient German never even entered my mind.

She had a job – as a Deutsche Bank trainee – lined up for early July. We would meet in Orlando and drop her at Nashville Airport. There we would meet the Spanish girl, appropriately called America.

America, from Saragossa, was twenty-one and had worked for us before. She was calm, patient, intelligent and excellent with the children. But her principal interests were youth culture (the latest bands and clubs – about which I knew nothing). I am a bald, thirty-

9

six-year-old with two kids. I liked America. But there was no danger there either.

In short, there was zero temptation. But that's unimportant. The point of this trip was to give my boys a fantastic summer and *full-time paternal attention*. I also wanted a great time – and to give Khelga three months to focus on her new job.

The day of departure arrived fast. After Khelga left for work we went to Gatwick. We were flying Virgin – the best airline for kids.

At the aircraft gate each boy received some 'Aviator Rations' and a Virgin Atlantic rucksack. We took our seats by a bulkhead (the best for small kids – there are no seats in front so they can lie on the floor) and the boys tore into their goodies. The rucksacks contained sunglasses and a Virgin Atlantic cap. For the next nine weeks (until Nicolai lost his hat in the Grand Canyon) they were walking adverts for Richard Branson.

The flight was surprisingly easy. The stewardesses were child-friendly and served special kids' meals. A personal TV monitor kept them amused. But after only two hours Nicolai, to my amazement, fell asleep. I padded Charlie's head with blankets, massaged his forehead and, to my delight, he dozed off too.

While they slept, I completed the American immigration forms. No, Nicolai had never been a member of the Nazi Party. No, he wasn't a convicted felon. No, he wasn't a drug user. Nor was Charlie. Nor was I.

By the time we landed they had slept for four hours. 'Welcome to Orlando,' said the captain, 'where it's a beautiful sunny day and the temperature is eighty-five degrees.' We disembarked and the Florida heat hit us. Nicolai refused to take his jumper off.

In our room at the Orlando Airport Marriot, Charlie was surprised by the beds. 'Why are there only two?' he asked.

'Because they're very big and two of us can share.'

'But we're not married . . . And I don't want to sleep with Nicolai.'

'Well, sleep with me then.'

'But I want to sleep with you,' said Nicolai.

So the three of us spent the first night of our trip tucked into one double bed.

3 The Motorhome Scene

A recreational vehicle (abbreviated to RV) is a 'motorised or towable vehicle providing temporary living accommodation'. Travel trailers (generally bigger than British caravans) are towed. Motorhomes, of course, are motorised.

Ownership is soaring in America. Not long ago RVs were associated with retired folk. Now the baby-boomers have caught the bug too.

Trailers start at ten thousand dollars. Smaller motorhomes go from around forty thousand (really basic models built on a pick-up chassis are cheaper). Top-of-the-range vehicles can reach a million dollars plus. Attractions are increasingly high levels of on-board comfort (microwaves, central heating and air-conditioning are standard, while luxuries include satellite TV dishes, global positioning systems, washing machines, central heating, power showers and internet hook-ups).

American roads are geared-up for large vehicles. Fuel is cheap and campers love the freedom of being able to take off without airline or hotel reservations. There are campgrounds all over the country and many of America's extraordinary natural spaces offer camping facilities.

I don't own a car because I've never needed one (and have always hated the idea of becoming dependent on one). I spent a decade travelling for a living, which meant I was hardly at home. Then I had children. Since then we've had other financial priorities. My father's ancient warning to me ('your hand will never be out of your pocket') given when I thought about buying one at seventeen, shows how *some* paternal influences stick (although these days he'd love me to buy a car — and gets embarrassed when I turn up with my kids on the bus). I must admit I wouldn't mind wheels, but living in Central London it's not hard without them (and when I really need a car I rent one).

Having always enjoyed camping, I thought touring in a motorhome would be the best way to cross America. Rental is easily arranged (many tour operators feature them) and they only require a standard driving licence.

A taxi took us to the Cruise America depot. I scanned the RVs in wonder – they looked enormous. We entered the reception area. Charlie's eye caught a line of gleaming Harley Davidsons. 'Daddy,' he suggested, 'why not hire a motorbike instead?'

'So, Mr Collins,' said the receptionist. 'Insurance...'

I settled for the best cover, with one million dollars worth of third-party liability. But coverage of the motorhome itself was restricted. Damage to the roof, the underneath, the interior, or any damage done while reversing, counted as 'negligence'. So, despite buying the most expensive policy available, much of the vehicle went uninsured.

'OK, Mr Collins, just watch this video – then you'll be ready to go.' She led me into a room, put on a film (full of camping tips I immediately forgot) and forty minutes later we were set.

The first thing I learnt was that driving a long vehicle meant allowing time to stop. I also learnt I couldn't pull out fast. Despite its six-and-a-half-litre V-8 engine, the RV lumbered slothfully from stop. To make matters worse on that very first drive, I didn't know where I was going.

Suddenly I saw a Wallmart. I needed some groceries so I pulled in and parked. This shop was vast – you could buy anything. I loaded up with groceries, cruised into 'Camping' (tossing in two kiddies' Disney sleeping bags), meandered around 'Motoring' (throwing in a *Rand McNally* – the authoritative US road atlas). Before long I was stuck in 'Toys' and the kids were testing bicycles around the store.

'Go on please, daddy – you did say, daddy...'

It was true I had promised them bikes and these 'Huffy Rockits', complete with stabilisers, were only forty-eight dollars each.

We emerged into the parking-lot with two full trolleys, bicycle wheels protruding from both of them. A Wallmart assistant pushed one trolley. 'Where y'all from?' she drawled.

'England,' I said.

'I guessed you were.'

She helped me load the RV. 'You drove this all the way from England?'

'Well, that's not actually possible,' I replied, amazed. 'England's on the other side of the Atlantic.'

'I kinda figured it was.' And I gave her a tip as the kids began peddling their brand new bicycles inside the giant motorhome.

For our first two nights I had reservations at Fort Wilderness. This is part of Disney World and probably the most child-friendly campground in the universe. (Incidentally, Americans call campsites 'campgrounds' – in the USA 'sites' are the spaces you camp on). Among the Fort Wilderness attractions were campground entertainments, plush sports facilities and Disney-character visits.

But first I had to reverse into my site, and remembering advice never to reverse in unaided (and with the threat of 'negligence' ringing in my head), I asked two teenage girls to be my lookouts. None of us was confident. Soon, one girl's dad appeared. 'So where do you want it, Bud?'

'Where do you suggest?' I asked. 'This is my first day in a motorhome.'

He directed me into the space and by the time I got out he'd begun connecting my hook-ups. 'OK, so this is your electricity...'

'Great,' I thought, 'I can switch on the air-conditioning and cool my beers.'

'This is your water – you're connected to the mains here, so you don't need your tank... And this is your sewer hose.' He opened a small cupboard on the side of the RV to reveal a curled-up, blue, spiralled pipe. 'How many are you? Three? Well, your sewer tank probably holds about twenty gallons. So you'll need to empty it once a week. I've got my wife, four kids and mother-in-law on board, so I like to do mine every day. But heh, they've got the most beautiful comfort stations in the world here so you should hardly use your sewer tank. Give me a shout if you need any help. You've got your hands full and we're just over there.'

'Thanks very much. Matthew,' I said and held out my hand.

'Kermit...'

He looked slightly wary, accustomed to predictable reactions. (What was his wife called? Miss Piggy?)

But straight-faced, I managed: 'Pleased to meet you, Kermit.'

'Pleased to meet you, Matt.' And he breezed back to his motorhome.

4 Character Dining

Despite the beautiful comfort stations we used our on-board facilities that night. Nicolai tested them first.

'Daddy,' he asked. 'Why haven't we got paper?'

'Oh, no! I forgot to buy some. You didn't need any did you?'

'No,' Nicolai answered. 'Because I used your sponge.'

Not mummy's face sponge? The one she had lent for our trip? I dived into the cubicle and found the loo blocked.

Why are small kids so entranced by bathrooms? A year or so before, I'd been in charge of Nicolai and trying to work. During a phone call he quietly disappeared. I found him in the bathroom attempting to clean his teeth with my disposable Bic razor (luckily the protective cap was on it). The phone rang a second time. Nicolai disappeared again. I found him in his favourite place – this time with a packet of digestive biscuits that he was merrily dunking in the toilet. (I grabbed the sodden things as he was about to savour them.)

I fished the sponge out of the motorhome loo and got the boys to bed. Next morning (after Kermit called to give me his old copy of *Woodalls*, a USA camping directory) we visited Disney's Magic Kingdom. This was not successful – the kids were too tired for great crowds of people. There's temptation in Orlando to cram in as much as possible, but with children you have to move at their pace. I could see already that many of my plans would have to be scrapped. We went back to the RV for a siesta but returned that evening for a 'character dining experience'.

'I'm sorry to have to do this to you,' said Clarissa, the seating hostess, at the Liberty Tavern (a restaurant where you could meet Disney-characters), 'but we've got a fifty-minute wait right now.'

We sat down with about forty other people. Outside, the weather was tropical but inside the restaurant it was freezing. Nicolai sneezed, Charlie started shivering and I was tempted to give up (and come back another day with thermals). But the kids wouldn't let me. They wanted their 'character dining experience'.

'Cute kids,' said the woman on my right. A small girl was sitting on her lap.

'Thanks,' I replied.

'On vacation alone?'

'Yes.'

'Very brave to come away with two kids.'

'You think so?'

'I do ... British?'

'Yes.'

'I guessed so ... Divorced?'

'Sorry ...?'

'You must be divorced, right?'

'No,' I said, surprised.

'Just having a break?'

'Yes.'

'Right ... Ever eaten with the characters?'

'No.'

'Well, your kids are gonna love it. It's a great experience. You seen any other character restaurants?'

'No.'

'Well, check out Chef Mickey – it's in the Contemporary Resort. They do fantastic breakfasts there.'

'Really?'

'You bet – and tomorrow we're going to eat with double-you-eye-en-en-eye-ee-tea-aitch-ee-pea-oh-oh-aitch in the Old Key West Resort.'

'Wow,' I replied, perplexed. 'Oh! Win ...' I began, when the penny dropped.

'Don't say it now – you'll spoil the surprise.'

Her husband returned with two older children. 'Larry, this British guy is all on his own in Florida with his kids. Neat, huh?'

'Uh huh,' grunted Larry.

'Number thirty-three,' Clarissa shouted. 'Margolis.'

'That's us,' said the woman and off the family went, beaming like lottery winners. To my left was another family. A mum, two kids and a grumpy dad. Suddenly a character appeared to those waiting – a taste of the treats we had in store.

'Look, Sal,' said the mum. 'It's Goofy – get his autograph. You, Marty – grab the camera, take his photo ...'

'Do we have to do this every time?' asked the grumpy dad. 'We've been on autograph and photo patrol all day. I can't take any more. Can't we just give it a break?'

Finally, Clarissa called our number. 'Forty-two. Collins.' And the three of us entered the restaurant. Tanya showed us to our table. Recognising her accent, I asked her whereabouts she was from.

'Novosibirsk – Siberia.'

And now here she was – a medieval English serving wench in Disney's Liberty Tavern. 'Das vedanya,' she said smiling, and waltzed away.

'Character dining' was joy for the kids. The food was a set menu of turkey, ham and beef *altogether* with trimmings, plus dessert and drinks. You could eat as much as you liked, but such was their excitement my boys could barely manage a cherry tomato each.

Having waited fifty extra minutes for dinner I was happy to concentrate on the food. But every time I tried, a character would arrive and pat me heartily on the back.

But the kids adored it. Goofy ran past us pretending to drive a car by using a plate as a steering-wheel. 'Can I give you a kiss?' asked Nicolai when he sat down at our table. He gave him a kiss. Minnie approached. 'Can I kiss you, Minnie?' He turned to me: 'Daddy, can we stay here all night?'

Charlie propositioned the shy, embarrassed mouse: 'Minnie, do you want to sleep with us? Do you want to come back to our RV?'

Nicolai got silly. 'Minnie, can I pour juice on your dress.'

The guys giggled naughtily. But the characters never spoke. Minnie looked suitably bashful and upset. Then she slipped away to other diners.

Mickey Mouse wasn't around that evening. Maybe he didn't work in the Liberty Tavern or maybe it was his evening off. But the boys kept asking where he was. I could see where this was leading. Despite the children eating practically nothing, and having a stomach full of wind myself, this meal had been such a success that I was already considering breakfast at Chef Mickey's, the restaurant recommended earlier.

But we made good use of the Liberty Tavern. Having arrived late, we were there as it closed. A handful of customers were finishing their meals and the characters were in the mood for fun. Goofy got so carried away with his steering-wheel that he crashed into a wall and smashed the plate. Then he dropped a glass. The kids thought that was great.

When he finally brought the 'check', our waiter Billy, a forty-something man dressed up in 'ye-olde-worlde' costume (frilly shirt, knickerbockers, silver-buckled shoes), said to me conspiratorially with a wink: 'So, dad and two boys, right? We dads have got to stick together. I'm a dad with two great boys, myself. Yes sir – two great boys...'

I left him a ten dollar tip.

'Character dining' was addictive. I made a reservation for breakfast at Chef Mickey's. That woman was right – the food was superb. Having eaten nothing the previous night, the kids were now ravenous and dived into the huge buffet range.

Starting with cereals, they followed up with pancakes, threw in some strawberries, knocked back orange juice, sampled different sausages, had another pancake, tried a few bananas, asked for more orange juice... And so it went on – each mouthful swallowed in between kisses for the characters.

Mickey, Minnie, Goofy, Pluto, Miko, Chip 'n' Dale were there. Nicolai tugged at Minnie's nose while Charlie asked her how she ate. 'Because you've got a plastic mouth... Yes, you've got a funny face, Minnie.'

Our next visit to the Magic Kingdom took in some children's rides but they were all we could manage. It was hot and crowded and distances between attractions were long for small kids.

After a siesta, we returned for the Grand Parade and fireworks' display. This was spectacular – the kind of thing we do in Britain every quarter century for events like a royal jubilee. At Disney World they do it every night.

We waved to the characters, then slipped away early to avoid the mass exodus.

5 Our First KOA

Our next base was the Orlando South KOA, part of the 'Kampground Of America' chain. I made a freephone call, reserved a site and headed there.

KOAs are useful. There are over six hundred in America and you'll find them near most cities. A free, user-friendly directory lists them state by state. They generally have a pool, playground and well-maintained facilities (clean bathrooms, launderette, recreation and washing rooms). They're highly commercialised but with kids it's convenient to plan trips around them.

Prices vary according to location but like most American campgrounds they usually offer a choice of spaces. Those with full hook-ups (from around twenty-five dollars) include sewer, electricity and water. (And sometimes cable TV too). Cheaper spaces (from around twenty-two dollars) lack on-site sewer facilities (which means, if you want to empty your waste tank, you drive to the campground 'dump station').

Probably as a delayed reaction to their jet lag, the kids' sleeping pattern now went mad. Nicolai and Charlie got up at four a.m. and I awoke to find them peddling through the RV on their bicycles, naked except for crash helmets.

They wouldn't return to bed so we had an early breakfast and decided to hit Seaworld. But we still didn't arrive until ten a.m. Cleaning the vehicle and getting the kids ready took forever. And that morning I made a typical novice's mistake.

'Sir! Sir!' screamed a hysterical-looking man running to the front of our vehicle. He was hopping around like a lunatic. 'Stop, sir! Now!' He looked insane. I wound down the window. 'Your hook-ups, sir! They're still connected!'

I thanked him and blushed. The sewer pipe was stretched to its limit. The electric plug pins were slightly bent but everything else was, thankfully, in order. I packed them up and set off.

Florida attractions are geared-up for motorhomes so we parked effortlessly in Seaworld's RV parking-lot and headed directly for the Shamu Stadium. It was packed but I found some seats and was warned we would probably get splashed.

I was explaining to the kids what a killer whale was when suddenly a huge, twenty-three-foot long, five-ton, black-and-white creature shot out of the pool, soared into the air and dived back into the water with a crashing splash. Nicolai was impressed: 'That's not a *penguin*, is it, daddy?'

After the show Charlie complained: 'But Shamu didn't splash us! I wanted him to splash me too.'

At 'Terrors of the Deep' we stared sharks in the eye. Nicolai was so captivated by them that he bumped into another toddler, knocking her over. She sobbed uncontrollably. 'Say sorry,' I ordered. Nicolai obeyed but then overcompensated by hugging her so tightly the father thought he was attempting to strangle her.

'Sorry, sorry, sorry,' said Nicolai.

'It's OK. She's got the message,' grunted the father. But Nicolai continued hugging her. 'I said it's OK. Will you leave her *alone?*' I scooped up Nicolai, smiled at the man and made for the dolphin show.

This was a beautiful event. The creatures performed so enchantingly they set off the Walter Mitty in me. 'Maybe I could go back to university,' I thought, 'and study marine biology and work with dolphins...'

After the show we bought Seaworld ice-creams in the form of whales. 'Will they taste of Shamu?' asked Charlie. Then we caught the baby dolphins' feeding time. That amused my own babies — although I did wonder whether yobs are born or made when Nicolai, to my horror, spat on a tiny dolphin as he popped his head up. But both boys were now hot and tired. We stared at some stingrays then left.

6 Hell's Angels, Gays and Sharks

Back at the campground two Harley Davidsons were parked in the space next to ours. The kids clambered on to them. 'Get off!' I bawled, 'or the owners will get angry.' The owners *were* angry. Two giant, bearded, Hell's Angels approached, menace in their eyes.

'Why have you got tattoos?' asked Charlie.

'Be quiet,' I muttered. 'And get off those bikes now...'

'They're cool,' said the first Hell's Angel. 'You wanna know why we got tattoos?... 'Cos we are just two dumb guys. You won't get tattoos when you're older, will you, son?'

'Yes, I will,' said Charlie. 'I'm going to get a Postman Pat tattoo.'

That evening, we met our other neighbours, the Mellows from Kansas: Maisie and Joe plus kids, Davie, Cindy and Trixie. The family had been to Disney World and were suffering deep shock.

'Did you know it was Gay Pride Day today?' asked Maisie. (I didn't.) She was fuming. 'We had *no* idea. Gays and lesbians had completely taken over. It was really unbelievable – eighty per cent of the visitors to Disney World today were homosexuals. And to think we'd planned this trip for months. The things they were doing were disgusting. And you should have seen the slogans on their T-shirts... Oh, my God! The trouble I had, explaining to the kids...'

'The gays had wanted to take over a family venue,' added Joe in a gloomy voice, 'to prove they could be the majority for a day. Well, they certainly put families into the minority. I demanded a refund and got it.'

While we talked our children played together. 'Do you have Gay Pride Days in England?' asked Maisie.

'Yes,' I said. 'But they've never taken over theme parks.' (I found it bizarre to think of gays taking over Chessington World of Adventures.) Once they had got gays off their chest they invited us into their motorhome. Both then began to wind down. We were soon discussing their RV history.

'Well, we started off with a little bitty one with no sewage

21

system,' said Joe. 'And just worked our way up. That was fourteen years ago, when Davie was a baby.' (Now they had a state-of-the-art thirty-two-footer.) They showed us around it, pointing out accessories such as the rear-view camera, satellite dish and global positioning system.

They were curious to see my rented vehicle, so I invited them over and we all, kids included, trooped into our motorhome. 'Did you drive this over from England?' asked Davie.

'No,' I replied, astonished to be asked that question for the second time in only four days. Did people here not know that the Atlantic Ocean separated Europe from America?

Joe talked about all the wonderful family trips they had made in their RVs. 'But we'll be very careful if we ever come back to Florida — to make sure it's not Gay Pride Day...'

They retired to their vehicle but two hours later, there was a tap on the door. I was in the bathroom. 'Answer that Charlie.' It was Joe.

'Is dad there?' he asked.

'He's wiping his bottom,' Charles informed him bluntly.

'Heh... I'll, I'll come back...'

'No, he's ready now... He's pulling his trousers up.'

'OK, er... Th–thank you Charlie.'

I rushed out apologising. 'Sorry about that, Joe. It's just that — being on my own — I have to watch them constantly, which means I can't do anything in private.'

'Course you can't, Matt — I understand. I really do... Anyway I just called to say we're leaving tomorrow. But before we go, if there's anything you need explaining about RVs, please don't hesitate to ask. You understand? Being a new camper and all that...'

I thanked him warmly, touched by the genuine camping camaraderie.

The following day was a lazy day, spent lolling by the pool and cycling around the campground (at least the kids rode — I had to run along behind). Joe, Maisie and family left before we were up but during breakfast outside we waved goodbye to our other neighbours. 'Cheerio,' said Charles, sounding extremely English, as the two bikers revved up.

'So long,' said the first one. 'Take care of your dad. And goodbye to you, little fella.'

'I'm not a feather,' said Nicolai. The men laughed and left on their Electraglides.

7 Yes, Jaws is Dead

By lunchtime the campground was empty, but by early evening there was a stream of new arrivals, with dozens of motorhomes towing cars. I was amazed. This was the first time I'd seen RVs pulling vehicles. Some towed huge saloons, others tiny compacts. The sight seemed to symbolise American self-indulgence. But only a few weeks later, after negotiating my vehicle through the narrow streets of Baltimore and paying twenty-four dollars to park the thing for an hour (because, the attendant informed me, I took up four spaces), I wished I'd been towing a car too.

By now we were short of clean clothes. We'd been away five days and I'd done no washing. The trip so far had seemed to consist of cooking, cleaning, taking the kids to theme parks, and amusing them on campgrounds. Not that I was complaining — it was just that time passed so fast. I had accumulated two bin-liners full of items awaiting washing. It was time to start recycling kit.

For our visit to Universal Studios, I fished out some soiled shorts and T-shirts from the bin bag. We didn't bother with underwear.

Having seen Seaworld's 'Terrors of the Deep', Charlie wanted to sample the 'Jaws' ride. I explained this was for grown-ups and suggested we stick to Barney. But he was determined. 'I want to see Jaws — I really do.'

'But it will be terrifying,' I advised. 'And Nicolai doesn't want to be terrified, do you, Nicolai?'

'Yes, I do,' he replied.

So we went on the Jaws ride. We boarded a small pleasure boat and sailed towards the 'Amity Island' coastline. To the kids' horror, the boat ahead suddenly sank. It disappeared underwater in seconds. Charlie and Nicolai were momentarily breathless. But when a giant shark leapt out and snapped at our boat, they jumped, yelping and terrified, up in the air. We sailed through an oil-storage yard. Jaws snapped again. The oil drums caught fire, flames shooting out towards the passengers. Both kids screamed. Then the yard exploded

— with an almighty boom. They jumped again. Their fear was intense. They trembled, screamed and clung for their lives to me.

'I want to get off,' wailed Charlie. Nicolai was so nervous he couldn't speak. I worried he might convulse. 'Let me off now!' howled Charlie. But we had to continue to the end of the ride. Panic-stricken, both kids clutched at me in terror and each time they saw the shark's tail they clung on even tighter, squealing. I felt the most irresponsible parent on the planet. The ride culminated with the skipper of our boat shooting it dead. The gun made a horrendous bang. When we got off the boat both kids were white with fear and trembling.

'Right,' I suggested heartily. 'Let's go and see Barney!'

Barney is a purple dinosaur with green spots dreamed up by a teacher from Texas. His show is a number one children's TV programme.

The Universal Barney Show was packed. A clown led us to the circular stage area and we awaited the star's arrival. Soon the audience was chanting. 'Bar-Ney, Bar-Ney.' All the adults and most kids were shouting. But we didn't participate. 'Are you going to sing for Barney, boys?' Both shook their heads.

You probably think they were suffering horrific psychological after-effects from the Jaws ride but I knew they had simply been overcome by an attack of British reserve.

Once in France I was at a Breton village disco when people started dancing 'Le Rock 'n' Roll'. Everyone – young and old – knew the movements. But I didn't and wouldn't join in. I just felt too British – too stiff, too reserved. 'Mon Dieu,' said the French girl I was with. 'You British are so *statique* it drives me mad...'

There at the Barney show, surrounded by frenzied Americans, my boys (despite being half-Russian) had suddenly become static and British. Americans young and old swayed, chanting, 'Barney.' There was singing, stamping and clapping but my two remained unmoved.

'Come on, Nicolai,' I said. 'Give Barney a clap.'

'Shut up,' came the terse reply.

When the purple dinosaur appeared they relaxed. He sang songs, introduced his friends and told stories. Then the show was finished and the audience fought its way to the stage to say goodbye. Next was the ET ride – a trip to the Extraterrestrial's home planet. Charlie and I liked the look of this.

A unique feature of the ride is that before you board, an operator feeds your name into a computer so that when it finishes ET personally says goodbye. But when it came to Nicolai the computer had a problem.

'What d'yah say his name was?' asked the operator.

'Nicolai.'

'Ain't got that – Nicola do?'

But before I had a chance to say that it certainly wouldn't, we were on our way to outer space. 'That's a girl's name!' I protested over my shoulder, pointlessly.

So as the ride ended, ET croaked: 'Goodbye Matthew... Goodbye Charlie... Goodbye *Nicola*...' My macho Nicolai was furious.

'I'm not a *girl*!' he fumed. (As soon as more Russians start doing Disney that computer will need to be reprogrammed.)

Seconds after we'd left ET, there was a tropical summer downpour. Within minutes, half the visitors were wearing ponchos – conveniently on sale everywhere. We looked at other rides but the walking, the heat, the crowds and the stimulation, had all taken their toll. Charlie was beginning to whine.

'I want some Coke.'

'You're not having any.'

'But I won't get hyper. And I want some Coke 'cos I'm really thirsty, I am.'

It was time to leave. But rain was still pouring down. By the time we'd reached the parking-lot the kids were soaked through.

Back in the motorhome, the only clean clothes I could offer were polo-neck jumpers and a choice of pyjama bottoms (somehow I'd packed eight pairs). The vehicle was now a mobile tip. The floor was filthy and slippery from wet shoes. Dirty pans and dishes lay in the sink and two bin-liners full of smelly clothes sat in passenger seats. It was three-thirty in the afternoon, ninety degrees outside and my kids were wearing pyjamas and polo necks. None of us was wearing shoes. If any cops stopped me I would die of shame.

En route back to the campground the kids spoke of Jaws.

'Is Jaws dead, daddy?' asked Charlie. 'Is he *really* dead?'

At the time of writing, I'm still reassuring them that, yes, Jaws definitely is dead.

8 Fort de Soto Park

Doing Florida's theme parks is like entering a series of giant TV sets with the colour and brightness turned to maximum. You're bombarded with stimuli and for a while enthralled. But then, with the crowds and the Florida sun, the rapture wears off and your energy fades. Having not taken the time to pace ourselves properly (i.e. leave a day between each visit) my boys (and I) were flagging. We were now ready to leave Orlando.

Our next reservation was at Fort de Soto Park in St Petersburg. America's parks are fabulous natural assets. The most famous are National Parks – areas of supreme beauty (like Yellowstone, Yosemite or the Grand Canyon) managed by the federal government. State Parks are administered by individual states and are often focused on sites of geological or historical importance. Like the national parks, they usually charge admission and offer facilities for campers. Fort de Soto is a county park – administered by Pinellas County.

St Petersburg itself, on Florida's Gulf Coast, has long been a popular holiday spot. In 1885 it was declared America's healthiest town. Today, the area's thirty-five miles of beaches are popular with Europeans recovering from theme parks. Its large number of resident, retired Americans earned Florida its nickname 'God's Waiting Room'. (Various billboards reinforce this impression: 'Fountain of Youth Plastic Surgery', 'Rad's Mobile X-Rays', and 'Chest Pain Center -- Because Your Heart Attack Won't Wait'.)

The town is promoted as only ninety minutes from Orlando. But that's in a Porsche, downhill, with the wind behind you and Jacques Villeneuve at the wheel. I was a novice British driver in a twenty-seven-foot-long RV. I'd been going ninety minutes when signs showed Tampa as twenty miles away (and that was another twenty from St Petersburg).

I was still driving when darkness fell. Then it started raining. I looked for the lights but couldn't find them. I fumbled with switches, trying to watch the road, and eventually the highway ahead became illuminated when I pulled out what I'd thought was the cigarette lighter.

We arrived at Fort de Soto at nine-thirty p.m. The campground gate was padlocked. But I saw a ranger's car and tooted my horn. A uniformed man, about six-foot-five tall, got out and approached me slowly with his flashlight. I told him I had a reservation, so he went into his office, checked my details and unlocked the gate. I followed him to my space then reversed. Leaves swished against the roof so I shouted out: 'Could you help me back up, please? This is bigger than things we drive in England.'

'What do you drive at home?' he asked when I was parked.

'I don't own a car.' The man scratched his head in disbelief.

Early next morning another ranger knocked at the door. 'Hello, Mr Collins,' he said, smiling, 'I heard you arrived last night. I just wanted to say welcome.'

He introduced himself as Trevor and said he had been in the beauty business — hairdressing — for over thirty years. He was a good advertisement for his trade — slim, dressed sportily in shorts and khaki shirt and crowned by a shock of thick brown hair. 'I'm retired from that now,' he added. 'But I love working as a ranger. It's such a beautiful place here.'

He mentioned that he'd wanted to see me because his family was originally from England. 'From Brad—*ford*,' he said (pronouncing the last syllable like the car). 'In York—*shire*.' (He made this last syllable rhyme with 'higher'.)

When I looked around I saw that Fort de Soto Park was indeed beautiful — a semi-tropical forest, tamed but not too sanitised. Camping neighbours around me were barely visible. The kids immediately loved it. We went for a cycle ride along one of the cycle paths used by elderly, tanned roller-bladers wearing Walkmans and fluorescent beachwear. 'How're yah doin'?' each one asked as they skated past. We then drove to the deserted, white sandy North Beach. I was already planning my return visit.

There was no one on the beach and the kids didn't have swimming trunks, so I undressed them, slapped on factor fifty and let them enjoy the scenery *au naturel*. As we waded in we noticed a warning sign. 'What does it say?' asked Charlie.

'It says there are sting-rays here and warns people to be careful where they walk.' Charlie dashed from the sea. From the beach he

29

asked about sharks. 'Well,' I said, lying in the warm, shallow water, Nicolai standing beside me, 'the only one here is the great white shark. It's fifty feet long with teeth so huge, that it not only eats people but whales and boats too! But it doesn't worry *me* because it doesn't like *grown-ups*. It only likes eating *little boys*.' I hummed the *Jaws* music. Nicolai fled. Charlie ran squealing up the beach.

'Only joking...' I called. 'That was daddy's silly joke.' Charles eyed me cautiously, unconvinced. I'd probably psychologically scarred him for the second time in twenty-four hours. Nicolai was more robust. 'Stupid man! You're not allowed to be a shark.'

After an hour, my kids' trust and jollity restored, we returned to the campground. Trevor helped us park in a waterfront space. But it wasn't appreciated. There was no beach by the water, just a steep bank where the boys kept wandering, and a sign which said: DON'T SWIM – DEEP HOLES.

I overcooked some sausages because I kept running out of the RV to make sure the boys weren't near the water. Then they complained that 'Daddy burns everything'. But they finished their lunch and I put them to bed. It was ninety in the shade and after swimming, cycling and fleeing sharks they were both tired.

Once they'd woken up the boys helped me with the washing in the campground launderette. Then we went for another cycle ride. We had salad for supper, a discussion about sharks and I put them to bed again.

Next day started badly. Nicolai woke up at five a.m. having had an accident. His Mickey Mouse sleeping bag was soaked. 'Flipping heck, Nicolai. Why did you have to wet the blinking bed?'

'I didn't wet it. I warmed it,' he maintained with dignity. I threw the sleeping bag in the shower and squirted shower gel all over it. Then after a good wash I spread the thing over the outside table to let it dry in the sun. By six-thirty Charlie was up too.

Later that morning I made a barbecue. I've always thought barbecues overrated (lots of effort for little reward). But I was doing this for my boys (they love fire) and because it's what you do when you camp. (And if I could watch them while I cooked lunch, maybe I wouldn't burn the food.) I smeared Buffalo Bill sauce on a piece of chicken and put it on the grill with several burgers.

We soon had an audience, a group of exotic birds – a pelican, two storks, some seagulls and a crow. 'They want to ride our bicycles,' said Nicolai. Unfortunately this wasn't so. I turned my back for a second and a stork put a burger in its beak. The kids and I stared open-mouthed. Two squirrels watched in amazement too.

Other birds, emboldened, now gathered. They looked at me and eyed-up the food. I felt harassed. More birds arrived. I began to feel like Tippi Hendren.

When we started eating (only burgers – the chicken wasn't ready), more feathered friends arrived. Birds attacked the scraps. Squirrels joined in too. I don't wish to sound paranoid but it soon seemed that every creature in the park was after us. Those on the ground stole our food, while those in the trees squawked and laughed.

The kids finished their lunch so I put them to bed. Then I returned to the barbecue. The chicken wasn't done so I went into the RV, did the washing-up, cleaned the floor and, an hour later, it was ready. I was no longer hungry but I put the meat on my plate and made a conscious effort to enjoy it. Suddenly the food held no interest at all. I'd noticed a black gash across the RV roof. I threw my chicken aside and climbed on to it.

To my horror, I found the white rubber roofskin had been slashed. There was a four-inch tear in it and the black waterproof sealant underneath had been smeared along the right-side plastic skirting.

How could I have done it? *Had* I done it? (Or was it something I'd missed at the Cruise America depot?)

I couldn't remember hitting anything. But Fort de Soto Park is a nine-hundred-acre-semi-tropical forest. Palm trees are everywhere. I must have hit one the previous night when I first tried to reverse into my space alone. Those rustling leaves must have been a branch. In the dark I'd missed the signs. I saw them extremely clearly now — BEWARE HANGING LIMBS.

While the kids slept I studied the insurance policy. I knew I wasn't insured against roof damage. But as I had taken the VIP Plus option (Vacation Interruption Plan Plus) I hoped that, just maybe, I was covered. But no. The small print stated clearly that even with VIP Plus I wasn't insured for damage to the roof or damage sustained while reversing. As this was *roof damage sustained while reversing* I was guilty of 'negligence' twice over.

I studied the Cruise America handbook and read up on 'Accidents and Maintenance'.

We don't wish to frighten you but these are some vehicle estimates:

ROOFSKIN PUNCTURE:	$500.00
REAR EXTERIOR – SKIRTING:	$500.00

What should I do? Have a go at DIY (and risk making an even bigger mess of it)? Or tell the company honestly what had happened? I chose the latter option.

I switched on the radio, turned the volume down, and tuned into a soothing soft rock station. A storm warning was announced: 'Heavy rain is expected in the St Petersburg area today as Tropical André blows in from the Pacific...' The vehicle was now not even waterproof.

I killed the radio and lay on my bed above the driving cab. The birds were still squawking – laughing at my misfortune. I closed my eyes and Nicolai woke up. I sighed, irritated. But no matter what mood you're in, how can you resist a three-year-old boy whose waking words are: 'Daddy, I love you'? He climbed up to the bunk and planted a kiss on my cheek.

The afternoon was going to be busy. Julia was arriving that evening at eight. As soon as the kids were dressed, I called Cruise America.

'Well, thank you so much for informing us of your problem,' said the woman on the phone. (That made me think some folks didn't bother.) She gave me the name of a local, company-approved service centre. Minutes later I set off.

It took me ages to find BILL'S RV CENTER AND REPAIR SHOP. It was a small place on a busy highway but when I arrived Bill himself (a seventyish man, slightly stooped but fizzing with energy and chuckles) was waiting. Cruise America had told him all about me. As the official repair company I worried he could charge what he liked. But Bill was fair. I told him what I was doing and burbled on about the budget nature of my project.

'The problem is,' I said, 'that I'm not earning a penny while I do this and with all the expenses... It was so unfortunate... Kids screaming in the back... No one to help me – and all in my very first week...'

Bill spoke like a father (well, like a paternalistic businessman). 'You know, son,' he said. 'These things happen all the time. We get so many folks comin' in here with damage done on their first RV trip. I mean, look at the most common accidents: holding tanks – they drag 'em off when they go up a kerb; overhead damage – they forget about clearance and get ACs removed; damage done reversing or going round corners... Lighting panels ruined or holes made in walls...You got off lightly my friend... And I tell you what – you'll be more cautious after this.'

'But, Bill, I was cautious... It's just that with only the kids on board...'

'I know, son, I know – don't you worry about it. But travelling with your kids across America... You are one hell of a lucky guy. Heh, you wanna beer?'

I said I would prefer the estimate first.

He climbed up his step-ladder and inhaled deeply. 'Well, there's good and bad news my friend. The good news is that we're not gonna have to replace your roof. But the bad news is that it's gonna cost you minimum two hundred and fifty dollars. It's a three- or four-hour job so you're gonna have to leave it overnight. But if you wanna save some cash – I've got an idea.'

He stepped down from the ladder, adjusted his yellow braces (they were calibrated into inches like a ruler), fumbled with his hearing aid and pushed back his natty, white, Gatsby-style cap. 'You can spend the night in my yard. Sleep in your motorhome – we don't get trouble. And if you're concerned, I'll ring the police and say there's a guy here with two young kids. You should be fine – we have never had a problem.'

I felt tempted. Insurance did not cover the roof. Had I been alone, I would have accepted. But here I was with my two tiny children – and a German au pair arriving that evening. I couldn't stay overnight in a downtown St Petersburg repair-shop yard. *Could I?* I declined his offer but told Bill to start the job as soon as possible and asked about nearby hotels.

'Well, the place down the road ain't bad. I'll call and see what they can do. Heh, Duane,' he shouted to his foreman, 'have some guys start on that roof now.'

'Yes, sir,' said Duane. And the boys and I entered the RV.

'Two minutes later Bill joined us. 'Good news,' he said beaming. 'We got you a corporate rate. They're gonna do it for forty-five bucks. I'll drive you over when we close.'

'Thanks Bill,' I said. 'But I've another problem – I've got to be at Orlando Airport in two hours. Can you help me find a rental-car?'

9   Fear and Chaos in St Petersburg

While Bill's receptionist (who doubled as his wife) enquired about rental-cars, Bill took a seat in my RV.

'You know, Matt, I was a salesman with NCR for years. I earned good money but I got worn out. I needed a vacation so I bought a used travel trailer and went up the eastern seaboard with my family... That's how I got into camping. Most campers I met were helpful and this introduced me to a different way of life...' I was interested in Bill's story but I was running late for Julia at the airport.

'You know I've got to be in Orlando very soon...'

'Don't worry, my friend — we'll sort you out... Anyway, as I was saying — I'd always been mechanically minded (I didn't have to invent the wheel or anything) so I learnt by freephone numbers, instruction manuals and courses...'

Duane, his foreman, approached the window and interrupted. 'You know, man, you might have a problem with a rental company as we can't find one with a car to spare.'

'You're joking...' I said.

'Nope — and it's too bad you can't take your RV 'cos we've pulled the roofskin back and now there's edging hanging off it and everything.'

The employees were beginning to pack up. Their working day was ending. I wanted to get to my hotel. Bill said he would take me immediately.

He went to inform his wife, and the boys and I walked over to his car. Some little girls were playing in the yard. 'You guys from England?' said the oldest one.

While we waited, she and Charlie chatted. The girl, who was about ten, was the daughter of a woman who worked for Bill. She said her name was Jennifer and that Duane was her mum's boyfriend.

'Heh, come here,' she shouted to her friends. 'This guy's from England and he speaks funny.'

Charlie and the girls talked while I waited anxiously for Bill. 'Is he your son?' asked Jennifer. 'Man, he's hilarious. He called me a smelly old woman.'

Bill finally arrived and we got in his car. 'You know I just love British TV,' he said as he started up the engine. 'We get a lot on PBS (Public Broadcasting Service), *Upstairs Downstairs*, *Monty Python*... Oh, boy, I love your TV.'

He dropped me at the hotel and I thanked him. 'See you in the morning. It'll be ready about eleven. Sleep well and don't worry, bud.'

We queued up to check in with half a dozen guests. A couple at the desk were haranguing the receptionist about a faulty TV. It seemed like we waited for hours. Finally we reached our room and I grabbed the phone. I was still confident that if I could only get a car quickly, then drive like Michael Schumacher to Orlando Airport, I could meet Julia in time.

But not a single rental-car was available in St Petersburg. I enquired about vehicles elsewhere – nothing was available remotely near. I enquired about a taxi to Orlando – it would cost a minimum of a hundred and fifty dollars but the companies had no drivers anyway. I enquired about flights – they would cost hundreds of dollars for the three of us (even though it was minutes away by plane). Finally, I searched for Julia's flight details – I wasn't going to be able to meet her.

But Julia's flight details were in my briefcase and I couldn't find that. I ransacked the room. The briefcase wasn't anywhere. I must have left it in the RV.

I phoned Bill's RV Center but no one was there. I looked up Lansford in the telephone directory (luckily I'd remembered Bill's surname) and called him at home.

'Hi, Bill, it's Matthew, the English guy – the one with the kids and the damaged RV... Listen, I'm really sorry but I've got a problem – I've left my briefcase in the RV. And it's got everything in it. You know: passport, tickets, that kind of stuff. I need a few things now and was wondering if I could collect it. Would that be OK?'

'Listen, Matt,' said Bill. 'Stay right where you are – I'll get one of my guys to bring it over...'

'Oh, that's great, Bill. Thanks very much. I really appreciate your help.'

'You're welcome buddy. See you tomorrow...'

I put the phone down and searched through the directory for

American Airlines. I dialled a number but an answering machine replied. It told me to redial during office hours.

I was frantically looking for another number when, to my horror, I noticed water seeping out of the bathroom. I slammed down the phone, ran across the room, opened the bathroom door and saw the kids giggling by an overflowing bath. Towels and an ice bucket were in it. The bathroom floor was flooded and the bedroom carpet near the door was soaked. So were the children.

'Stupid, stupid boys!' I yelled. 'Look at this bl–inking mess you've made.'

'*Please* don't say blinking,' begged Charlie.

The only other outfits I had were more pyjamas. So I took off their wet clothes and got them ready for bed even though it was only six pm.

I went back to the telephone, looked up American Airlines again and dialled the other number. An automatic message took my call. Seemingly years later it gave a list of options. Finally I got the one I wanted: 'If you need to speak to an operator, please dial zero.' I dialled zero. 'Please stay on the line – an operator will be with you soon.'

An operator wasn't with me soon so I rang London. 'Khelga,' I shouted, 'it's me – listen... We've had a problem with the RV and I'm not going to be able to meet Julia. Tell her if she rings that I'll find her an airport hotel.'

Khelga exploded. 'What do you mean you're not able to meet her? She'll go berserk. If you're not there I won't be surprised if she takes the next plane to Germany...'

'Listen, Khelga, calm down... And try and calm Julia down if she rings. I can't talk long but I need her flight details.'

'Why the bloody hell do you need her flight details?'

'Because I've left them in my briefcase which is in the RV and that's in a repair shop which is unfortunately closed for the night...'

'What! I knew this trip would be disastrous...'

'Khelga, shut up and give me her flight numbers...'

Moments later she returned to the phone and gave me the required information.

'Thanks... Now take down our number... I've got to go... We're in a hotel and the kids are flooding the bathroom again. *Get out of that bathroom!* I screamed.

I scooped up the kids, threw them on a bed, looked up hotels in the telephone directory, waited interminably to speak to a human being at the Holiday Inn Central Reservations number and booked a room for Julia at the airport. I was just about to try American Airlines a third time when the phone rang. It was Bill's guy. He couldn't find my case. I told him it was in the shower. 'Yes, I know it's a strange place to keep a briefcase but I put it there to hide it – in case someone breaks into the RV.'

Minutes later the man was at the door. 'Thank you so much, that's great,' I said taking the briefcase. 'I really appreciate your trouble.' I put my hand in my pocket and took out a few bucks to show my appreciation. Then I ran back to the phone and tried American Airlines again.

This time I hung on (the voice reassured me my call was important) and eventually spoke to a human. 'Hello, I'm supposed to be meeting someone arriving from London – via Miami. Her flight number to Orlando was AA456. Her name's Bley – Julia Bley. She's a nineteen-year-old German girl.'

'Uh–oh!' said the man. 'That sounds familiar. Wait one minute please.'

I hung on nervously and he came back. 'Er ... Ms Bley's flight has already come in. She's with our people and is pretty upset ...'

'Right,' I said, 'could you give her a message, please? Could you tell her Matthew rang and that I'm really sorry I couldn't meet her but we had a major RV problem ... Could you also tell her to call me.' And I gave him my hotel phone number.

Two minutes later the phone rang. It was Khelga. 'Matthew, what's happening? Herbert (Julia's father) has just rung and said Julia's incredibly upset because she hasn't a clue where you are. What the bloody hell have you been up to?'

'Right ... I've got her a reservation at the Holiday Inn at Orlando Airport. There's a free shuttle to the hotel. Ring Herbert, get in touch with Julia and tell her to take the shuttle to the H–O–L–I–D–A–Y ... I–N–N ...' I enunciated it as slowly as I could without further enraging Khelga. 'The Holiday Inn at Orlando airport, OK? This is the booking reference – you got that? Thanks ... Right ... Bye ...'

I put the phone down and it immediately rang again. It was Julia – in tears. 'Julia, I'm sorry – it's been a bloody awful day ...'

'It's been a bloody awful day for *me* ...'

'I know ... Listen ... You've got a reservation at the Holiday Inn at

Orlando Airport. Take the free hotel shuttle bus from outside the arrivals hall and ring me again when you get there. Julia, I'm really sorry... We had a problem with the RV. We hit a tree and the roof's damaged... And then there were other problems too. The H–O–L–I–D–A–Y... I–N–N... OK...? This is your booking reference... Julia, I'm really sorry. But it's been a nightmare day. Ring me when you get to your hotel and have dinner or whatever you want. Order anything on room service. Ring your dad and Khelga from your room... I'll pay the bill... Speak to you in a few minutes... OK, Julia? Try and calm down. Everything's OK. I'm really sorry... Bye...'

I lay down on the bed, shut my eyes and let the guilt wash through me. Julia was the last person I would ever have wanted to let down. She had been with us for six months and was the most wonderful, conscientious, reliable au pair. And I wasn't even there to meet her at the airport.

Suddenly I was thumped in the stomach. It was Nicolai. 'Daddy, I'm hungry, I'm really hungry.'

'I'm hungry, too,' chipped in Charlie.

'All right,' I conceded. 'Let's have some room service.'

But this hotel did not provide room service. The receptionist informed me that the nearest restaurant was Denny's – a block away. So I picked up the boys – both in pyjamas – and carried them across two parking-lots to the restaurant.

'How're you guys today?' asked a beefy, six-foot-something waitress. Her name badge said 'Brandy'. Within seconds she'd slapped crayons and paper on the table and within minutes delivered our food.

The kids' drinks were served in 'Children of the World' beakers.

'You can keep those,' she smiled.

'Can we keep this too?' asked Charlie, thrusting a side-plate down his pyjama trousers.

Half an hour later we were done. The boys were full of burgers and I was feeling pretty sick myself. The kids' night attire had not intrigued anyone. In fact the place was filled with weird types.

It was this which made me ponder the walk back to our hotel. I rarely worry when travelling alone. But with two tiny children... It was now dark outside and I didn't like the idea of carrying the boys across two poorly lit parking-lots.

'Excuse me,' I mumbled to our muscular waitress. She looked tough enough to see off any trouble. I plucked up my courage and dived in: 'If I gave you an extra tip, would you mind escorting me back to our hotel. It's across those two dark parking-lots. It's just that I'm British and alone with my two children... And...'

'What's that, sir?' she asked, proceeding to spell out my question at full volume: 'You want me to walk with you across those parking-lots? Are you really that afraid of trouble?... Let me tell you, sir, you have got nothing to fear here. I have not experienced one single mugging in all the years I've worked at Denny's.'

'OK,' I said, meekly, eyes to the ground. 'Thanks... It's just that, you know, being British and all that — we're still adapting to America...'

I paid our bill and slipped sheepishly out of the restaurant. Then I sprinted with my offspring to our hotel room and didn't pause for breath until the door was double-locked and chained.

10 Another Near Disaster with Julia

The following morning I had to suffer the humiliation of going back to our only option, Denny's, for breakfast. At least there was no worry walking there – the Florida sun made the parking-lots look heavenly after the menace of the night.

But, just as I had feared, Brandy was on breakfast shift. 'So, Mr Britisher,' she said, leading us to our table. 'Get back to your hotel alive?'

'Yes,' I replied, feeling like the wimpiest Englishman ever to have crossed the Atlantic.

'No, we don't get a whole lot of trouble round here. Just the occasional parking-lot murder – heh, I'm joking! Now what can I can get you folks for breakfast?'

'Did she say murder?' asked Charlie.

After breakfast we paid the 'check' and said a final farewell to our waitress (who had to score one last point – 'Now, you don't want me to see you across those two parking-lots this mornin', do you, guys, huh?' More laughter...) we returned to our room and I phoned Julia. Then we collected the RV. The repair came to two hundred and sixty-seven dollars, including tax (which meant that with two hotel bills, food, phone and extras, the 'swish of the leaves' had cost around six hundred bucks).

I shook Bill's hand and thanked him for doing the job quickly. 'Farewell, Matthew,' he said. 'And enjoy your boys.' He was with a customer and explained my trip to her.

'Travelling across America with his kids and *without* his wife?' she repeated, obviously mystified. 'Well, he's certainly *brave*.' (For which I read: 'What a nut!')

We arrived at Julia's hotel around lunchtime. 'Miss Bley?' said the receptionist. 'She's over there.' And I saw Julia slumped in a chair, looking understandably fed up. I didn't like Julia to be fed up. Her German organisational skills were much appreciated in our chaotic Anglo/Russian household and I liked to keep her as sweet as possible. We boarded the RV, I enthused about the joys to come and we headed north.

Unfortunately I got stuck on a road going east and two hours later was worried sick when I noticed how little fuel we had. How stupid I had been for not filling up! I still wasn't used to this vehicle's extraordinary petrol consumption (ten to the gallon). During the next half-hour, the gauge sank through the red warning zone. We were on a highway with trees and swamp around us. There were no signs or turnings. Soon the gauge had fallen below the warning zone.

I held the cruise control at fifty-five mph and willed every droplet of gas into the engine. After twenty more minutes, the sun set, traffic became minimal and still there weren't any signs. But I didn't say anything. The last thing Julia needed was another crisis and I was loath to inform her of the risk we stood of running out of petrol on a quiet Florida highway in the middle of nowhere at night-time.

'Please God,' I muttered, 'don't let me run out here.' Julia caught my eye in the overhead mirror and I smiled stupidly, as I prayed frantically. 'Please, God, don't let us run out of gas. Not here — please, please, God.'

I dropped my speed to fifty and continued to psyche fuel from the tank. I was now also sending vibes to the engine. 'Come on, baby, you can do it. Come on now, baby, please be good to me...'

More minutes passed and I became convinced it was just a matter of seconds before we ground to a dismal halt. But twenty miles from Titusville I saw the light. Like St Paul on the road to Damascus, I saw a brilliant sign ahead. It gave a list of options. Gas was one of them — a mere four miles away.

I continued at fifty mph, kept up the psyching and more signs appeared: GAS – 2 MILES; GAS – 1 MILE; GAS – ½ MILE. Then we were there. We had made it! Never had the Texaco logo looked so beautiful. 'Thank you, God!' I said, as we pulled on to the forecourt. 'Engine, I love you — you are gorgeous.' When I removed the filler cap the tank hissed crazily. I must have had an eggcupful to spare.

All this time Julia and the children had been in blissful ignorance. Charlie's only interest had been to get as many of Julia's furry toys out of her suitcase as possible. Oh, to be a boy of four.

I filled the tank with every last drop of gas I could squeeze into it. Then I paid the cashier, beaming idiotically as I handed over the money and thanking her excessively for her help. I truly appreciated being at the gas station. She must have thought me a jerk.

By nine p.m. I had had enough of driving. Julia was also, understandably, shattered. So we looked up the nearest KOA in the directory and stopped at the campground in St Augustine.

11 Heading North

St Augustine, founded by Spanish adventurer Pedro Menendez de Aviles in 1565, was the first European colony in North America. Today it's a well-preserved Spanish colonial centre. It also has several fine beaches.

I wanted to explore. But my boys loved the campground — especially the swimming pool. They made friends who lent them some 'noodles', long strips of brightly-coloured foam used as buoyancy aids. But Nicolai also wanted their masks and fins.

'Put them back,' I ordered, as he laid into the family's poolside pile.

'It's OK,' said the father. He was a relaxed, mustachioed, Burt Reynolds type. 'Where y'all from?' he asked. The answer led to an invitation for coffee and cookies at his RV.

It turned out he lived in central Florida with his second wife. They had seven kids between them (ranging in age from three to eleven) and spent most weekends in their motor home. All our kids got on famously (mine got to play with their toys — theirs got to hear mine speak). Jack, the father, enthused about British cars and motorbikes.

When it was time to move on, I was reluctant to leave. 'So, eleven weeks on the road?' he said, as I started the engine. 'Well, you're gonna be an RV professional by the time you reach LA. Have a safe trip, buddy.' We pulled away. Everyone waved.

That was my first intense driving day. With food and rest-room breaks, we spent eight hours on the road. We were heading north on I-95, part of the 'Interstate' system dreamed up by President Eisenhower in the 1950s.

The straight, wide roads are useful for covering long distances rapidly. And they're simply numbered. Even-numbered Interstates usually run east-west. Odd ones run north-south.

But after British motorways they take some getting used to. Apart from varying speed limits (one minute it might be seventy mph, the next fifty-five), Americans frequently change lanes. They also overtake on both sides.

On I-95 I was struck by the amount of roadside carnage. Squirrels, armadillos, dogs and cats, squashed by traffic and in various stages of decay (from freshly killed to several weeks old), were among the natural casualties. Man-made detritus was usually chewed-up bits of tyre.

Cars overtook me. Motorbikes streaked by. One was a red Honda Goldwing with matching side-car combination. A mah and pah rode the bike, goggles only on their heads. Two helmeted boys sat in the side-car. They must have shot past at eighty.

But speeding trucks made the most terrifying impression. Giant, gleaming road trains crept up suddenly, their airstream first causing the RV to veer, then sucking us towards them as they thundered by.

For the first time on our trip I noticed cars without Florida registration plates. One from Ontario overtook me. Then, to my amazement, a car from Alaska passed. We were heading north. It felt great to be leaving tourist territory.

Generally I ticked over at sixty mph. The RV's cruise control made maintaining speed effortless and fuel consumption was minimised. Sixty-five felt supersonic and at anything over seventy the RV vibrated frighteningly.

We crossed our first state border and headed into Georgia. Then the clouds opened and warm rain hammered down. I seemed to be the only driver obeying the speed limits. During the next hour we passed four accident scenes. They were attended by police dressed in shorts and Canadian Mountie-style hats. Some were also wearing ponchos. These ended at the knees, exposing the cops' legs and giving the impression they were naked beneath the ponchos. Beside two wrecked cars a cop waved, Canute-like, trying to make traffic slow down. Few motorists obeyed the bizarre, cape-clad figure.

My only diversion was into Savannah. Restoration work on the old houses and mansions of this former cotton exporting centre (which declined after the Civil War and the crash of cotton prices) began in the 1950s. Savannah's beauty is on a par with that of New Orleans and Charleston but the city never *used* to be on the obvious tourist trail. Two things changed that: the movie *Forest Gump* (Tom Hanks's bench scene was filmed in Chippewa Square) and a book (now a film), *Midnight in the Garden of Good and Evil* (an evocative, local tale of murder and intrigue).

But we arrived late and the children were weary. My RV driving skills were still so limited that I got tangled up in one-way systems.

The kids began to howl so I drove out of town.

I carried on driving and soon saw a WELCOME TO SOUTH CAROLINA sign. I was racing north because of something I haven't mentioned before.

In just over a week I was due to go to Athens. Not Athens, Georgia. But the original Athens, Greece. Yes — Greece, Europe! I had been booked, long before finalising this trip, to host a travel-industry conference there. If I had started this trip after Greece, I would have lost three weeks of our precious summer.

The plan was to hurtle up to Washington DC where Khelga would fly in to meet us. I would dash to Greece and fly back to Washington. Khelga would then return to London.

Shortly after crossing the border we pulled into the South Carolina Welcome Center. Nicolai woke up. His seat was soaked with sweat so I dressed him in fresh clothes, and we guys trooped off to the rest room. I was getting into Kerouac mode (although Jack's characters broke for 'peeesss stops' while we had to go for little 'wee-wees').

Back on the road my passengers fell asleep leaving me free to tune into the radio *and* concentrate on the highway. Non-stop audio messages competed for attention. *'Get $3,000 cash when you buy a new Ford GT... Happy Father's Day from Larry's Golf and Tennis Center...'* There were numerous billboards: *The World's Greatest Firework Store... Mama's Italian Place...* And endless bumper stickers: *For a Healthy Relaxing Massage Call 785 RUBB... I Still Miss My Ex-Wife But My Aim Is Improving...*

The drive was calm. Then Nicolai opened the door — at sixty mph. Until this point he would only sleep when sitting in the front seat which reclined. Outside Savannah I'd belted him into it on his booster seat. Then he'd dozed off. But shortly afterwards quietly woken up. He pulled on the door handle and a swirling rush of wind filled the motorhome. I leaned over, trying to shut the rattling door — but failing. I looked in my mirror, stopped dead on the verge, slammed it shut and yelled. For the next few days I had visions of Nicolai falling out of the speeding RV. The vehicle had no child locks. Neither boy would ever sit in the front again.

I went on and on to both of them about the dangers of touching the door when we were moving. For half an hour Nicolai chanted mantra-like: 'I promise I won't open the door, daddy, I promise I won't open the door again...'

12 Hilton Head and Harvey *Nickels*

Shortly after the door scare we arrived at Hilton Head, an island off the South Carolina coast connected to the mainland by a highway. I'd heard about its glorious beaches and had earlier booked a treat – a night in a HH hotel. But Charlie didn't appreciate the gesture. 'I want to sleep in the RV...'

The Shoney's Inn manager was English, from Southampton, but the kids simply did not want to stay in his establishment. I couldn't believe their ingratitude.

I suggested a meal in the restaurant – another treat. But no – the kids wanted to eat in the RV. So I proposed a compromise (which the hotel would have hated) – that we take some food out of the motorhome and eat it in our hotel room.

As I approached the vehicle a security man asked me to re-park (it was Saturday evening and I was taking up five spaces). He guided me to the side of the hotel and promised to watch the RV that night. I grabbed some provisions and scuttled back to our room. We ate our food but the children refused to settle. They wanted to sleep in the RV.

Like vagabonds, we slipped out of the hotel room, walked around the building and into the passage where the RV was parked. I spread the duvets on the over-cab bunk and the kids dozed off instantly. Julia spent the evening alone.

Next day, we checked out and looked for a campground. There were two on Hilton Head but they were camping 'resorts', run as 'condominiums', meaning campers bought a permanent campsite space which they could rent out when they weren't there. The problem this created was that campground staff were not permitted to recommend spaces to passing campers.

'So where do you think would be best for kids?' I asked the receptionist at the Hilton Head Island Motorcoach Resort.

'I can't say, sir. You see, each site is individually owned but everything is managed equally by us – so we're not allowed to show preference. Just drive around and tell us which empty space you like.'

We found one near the pool. This campground was certainly more up-market than KOAs. The grass was manicured, the rest-room floors pristine and state-of-the-art RVs were everywhere. Some looked like the kind of things you imagine bands use when they go on tour but instead of having hell-raising rock stars as occupants, most contained elderly, sedate couples.

I got talking to a man in the swimming pool. His name was Fred, and he was a schoolteacher from Wisconsin. 'No, sir, *I* couldn't afford to buy a site here. You know, apart from the fortune it costs people for their space, they pay service charges every quarter. It's real expensive, buying into this. And that's apart from the RVs themselves. You see that Provost over there? Man, that's probably worth almost half a million dollars...'

'But why do people buy such expensive, depreciating assets?' I asked naïvely. 'Why don't they just buy a house?'

'These people have that stuff already. Second, third homes, boats, that kind of thing. Some of the folks here are seriously rich.'

That afternoon Fred took tea with us. Then he explained American coinage to Charlie: 'Well you see that one there – that's called a quarter. That's worth twenty-five cents. This one's a dime – that's worth ten cents. And this one is five cents. It's called a nickel.'

'You mean a Harvey Nichol?' asked my son. I had never realised what frighteningly urbane little Londoners I'd produced.

'What's that?' asked Fred.

'Nothing,' I said. 'Charlie's confused. Harvey Nichols is a famous clothes shop in London – [and was] one of Princess Diana's favourite stores. But we go there occasionally on Saturdays because I adore the food hall and it gives away free samples. The kids love it – they go round munching any free stuff they can. And it's all high quality, of course.'

'One of Princess Diana's favourite stores, huh?' mused Fred, impressed. 'Man, that must be something...'

In the evening we took a Dolphin Cruise but it was disappointing. We only saw one dolphin, from a distance and for seconds. The most interesting part of the commentary was when the skipper informed us that we were sailing on America's Intracoastal Waterway, built to protect ships from potential attack. 'And completed in the late 1930s... Just in time to see off the German U-boat threat.' Julia rolled her eyes.

During the night there was a violent Hammer Horror-type thunderstorm. The kids awoke and were alarmed by the noise and lightning. But early next morning it was sunny, so we swam. The pool was full of frogs — hundreds of them, all sizes. Nicolai found a tiny one on the edge of the pool.

'Look, daddy, look,' he said, excitedly. 'What a sweet little frog.' It was barely an inch long. 'I love this frog, daddy. He's so sweet.'

'Yes, it is sweet,' I said.

'I know, daddy — let's kill him.' He stamped on the ground but I flicked it away just in time.

GOD LOVES YOU Y'KNOW... DO YOU WANT TO MEET HIM ?

After lunch we checked out. This campground wasn't geared up for kids.

Driving towards Charleston on Highway 17 (a US Highway is one down from an Interstate), I began to feel that we'd left America and entered some far off third-world corner. Poorly dressed hawkers sold watermelons, squash, leather and wicker work. Behind them were lush plantations. It was Sunday and the road was dotted with churches — Pentecostal, Episcopalian, Baptist — all full of locals dressed in their Sunday best.

While my passengers slept I switched on the radio and station-hopped. 'Fox 106.1,' said a jingle. 'Rock 'n' Roll minus all the weird stuff. When you listen you know what you'll get.' Another was more adventurous: 'Zee 102.2, rock you grew up with *and* the modern stuff...'

After a long drive we arrived at the Charleston KOA. We found a supermarket, went shopping, had supper and put the kids to bed.

Next morning we ventured downtown. We parked the RV at Central Station and took a trolley bus to the centre. 'You know, some of these buildings are a hundred years old,' a lady passenger told us.

'I do know,' I said. 'And my house is a hundred years old too...'

'Well, you folks are lucky to have all that history. I'm going to Europe someday.'

But Charleston also has a rich history. The Civil War started here in 1861 and the Historic District is full of mansions adorned with ironwork wrought by slaves. One third of America's slaves came through the city. The war was essentially a fight over slavery — between the Northern states remaining in the Union and the Southern Confederacy of slave-owning states which seceded from it. The Confederacy lost. One in four of its male adult population died and the economy of the South was destroyed. General Robert E. Lee surrendered on 9 April 1865. Days later President Lincoln was assassinated.

After a city tour I bought Nicolai some trainers. He needed summer shoes and, reduced to eighteen dollars, they were a bargain. Unfortunately the shop had nothing suitably cheap in Charlie's size. The salesman searched helpfully but without success. Charlie was furious. Nicolai glowed as he strolled out in his Reeboks.

'You have a really great day,' said the salesman.

'And you have a really horrible one!' bawled my charming son.

13 Myrtle Beach

Driving north to Myrtle Beach, I switched on the radio and station-hopped again. Suddenly I heard a familiar voice. It was Frank Muir singing some music-hall ditty. 'Radio 4? It can't be . . .'

But it was. 'You've been listening to music from the BBC presented by Steve Race,' said the English voice at the end of the programme. 'Maybe I'll get *The Archers*,' I thought. But Steve Race was followed by a local announcer: 'Don't miss tonight's Crosby, Stills and Nash benefit concert. This is South Carolina public radio.'

I station-hopped again and came across music which seemed momentarily appropriate: 'Driving along in my automobile . . .' Except that my baby wasn't beside me at the wheel. I had two kids and a German au pair in the back of a twenty-seven-foot-long motorhome. I flicked to another station: 'We're going to Cali–fornia where the weather's warmer.' That was more my thing. Then the DJ said: 'You're listening to Oldies Cool FM.' I flicked channels and tuned to a rap station.

Within seconds of pulling into our site at the Myrtle Beach KOA we'd been joined by an elderly figure in a sailor's cap. 'So where are you from in Washington?' he enquired.

'Pardon?'

'Your licence plate – your motorhome's from Washington State.'

'Oh, is it?' I hadn't noticed. 'We rented this in Florida. I'm from England and she's from Germany.'

'From Germany? Whereabouts?'

'Cologne,' said Julia.

'Cologne, huh? Well, I gotta lot of respect for Germans. You were mighty clever in World War II.'

Julia smiled wearily. Since arriving in Britain only seven months before, she had become used to mention of the war. She had heard more talk (and seen more programmes) about it in that short period than she had previously heard in her entire life.

And now, within only seconds of meeting her, Frank from Ohio, was talking about 'WWII'.

'Yes, I'm seventy-five and I was drafted. I got to France and Germany in 'forty-five but I haven't been back to Europe since. I guess things have changed a lot?'

'I guess so,' said Julia.

'I'd sure like to go back.'

'Well, you would find things very different,' she smiled. 'But I think you would like Germany now.'

'I reckon I would,' said Frank.

'Will you come here,' yelled a female voice. It was Frank's wife. 'I'm sorry,' she said. 'I just can't stop him, walking around, boring other campers.'

'He's not boring us,' Julia said kindly.

'She's from Germany,' said Frank.

'I'll take him away,' said Frank's wife.

At the swimming pool we enjoyed more attention. 'What does he speak?' asked a girl about Charlie.

'English,' I said.

'Some accent, man!' She told her friends who gathered round. We were unique – the only Brits in the pool among dozens of vacationing Americans. The boys were soon borrowing rings, balls and inflatable toys. They were in danger of becoming (thoroughly) spoilt – too used to being lent other children's possessions merely because they were British. Most American kids seemed friendly, open and willing to share – often more pleasant than my little hustlers.

Myrtle Beach is a massive, sprawling, family-oriented tourist town – an American combination of Blackpool and Benidorm. It's a twenty-six-mile-long line of water parks, beaches, crazy golf, funfairs and bungee jumps. In the evening we went to a funfair.

I bought some coupons to use on the kiddy rides. These were a huge success. Riding mini helicopters, fire engines and motorbikes, the boys had a fantastic time. Then the heavens opened and customers disappeared. As so few remained, the young ride attendants didn't now even bother collecting coupons. We drifted happily from one ride to the next, trying out whatever rides we fancied.

While the boys sailed two speedboats on a roundabout I spoke to the girl attending it. She was gorgeous – black, about twenty – but wearing a pendant that said: '100% BITCH'.

'That true?' I said, nodding at the pendant. She fluttered her lashes and purred. 'Oh my word – you are *so* coo–ool...'

Now 'cool' is *not* a word often used about me. In fact, this was very probably a first. (I'll never be invited to one of Tony Blair's 'Cool Britannia' soirées.)

'Wow,' I thought excited. 'How could my boring accent produce such a magical effect? If I didn't have the kids with me, I could pull anyone.' So here's some advice: If you're a young lad, off to America – go where other Brits are a rarity.

I later met a Brit manning the kiddies' motorbikes. But she was female – a Lancashire lass, taking American Studies at a university in England and in Myrtle Beach on a student exchange. 'No, I didn't think I'd spend my year in America working at a fairground, either,' she complained. 'It's hardly cultural. I might as well have gone to Alton Towers...'

Back on the road (after filling up in Myrtle Beach with the cheapest gas I'd seen so far – ninety-nine cents a gallon), we continued north. Driving with the window down, I asked Julia to fetch my hat. She put her hand in a cupboard, fished out my panama and passed it over. I put the hat on and a nauseous whiff hit me. I removed it, sniffed it and nearly passed out.

Julia poked her head inside the cupboard and pulled out a green-hued nappy. 'Ugh!' she shrieked. 'This must have been in here for weeks.' (After Nicolai had wet his bed I'd put nappies on him for a while.)

Several hours later, another evil odour filled the air. I parked in a rest area, opened the freezer door and a hideous stink escaped. The culprits were foul-smelling chicken breasts. Removing them, I found equally disgusting slimy steaks, soggy beefburgers, limp sausages, sweaty pizzas and horrible, slippery, smelly fish. I had been forgetting to switch on to gas power whenever we were away from mains electricity. About a hundred dollars' worth of food was ruined.

'Shhiiiitt!' I cussed.

And then a voice cooed: 'You're listening to the family radio station – Magic 107.2. No filth, no bad language, no blue jokes – conversation you won't be embarrassed to listen to with your kids.'

'Blinking hell!' I spat.

'Please don't say *blinking*,' pleaded Charlie.

I slung out the food and we continued our journey. That evening we arrived in Virginia.

14 Nearing the Capital

We spent the night at Petersburg KOA (obviously popular with northerners heading south for winter — WELCOME SNOWBIRDS said signs), then started driving again. I played 'spot the most stupid bumper sticker' (candidates included: *Save The Planet — Kill Yourself, Gun Control Is Using Both Hands, Mean People Suck, My Son Goes To College — And So Does My Money* and — on a sparkling, large, new RV — *We're Spending Our Kids' Inheritance*). The boys and Julia sat at the dinette table and drew or did jigsaw puzzles. Or we would all simply chat. Later in our trip we met plenty of families who kept their kids amused with non-stop videos. 'How do you stop yours getting bored if you don't even have a video?' people asked.

'We talk,' I said. And we did. About anything — American cars, RVs, motorbikes, London, Germany, Jaws, John Major, Tony Blair, other road-users... ('That driver was a prat, wasn't he?' said Charlie, when he sensed that one had angered me.) The only thing I could never explain was distance.

'Can we go to Hyde Park?' asked Nicolai.

'Of course we can't. Hyde Park's in London. We're in America — a very, very long way from London.'

'All right,' said Charlie. 'Let's go to Universal Studios and do the Jaws ride again. That's in America, daddy...'

After a morning's drive we stopped at a campground in Fredericksburg. Khelga was due to arrive in Washington DC two days later and I was flying to Athens the day after. As Khelga doesn't drive, and as the campground provided a bus to a DC train service, I thought it might make a convenient base. But I also thought I should recce the Washington area to see if there were any others closer. So, I phoned a car rental company, a rep collected me, took me to the depot — and I drove back in a white Ford.

'Are we going to live in *that* now?' asked Charlie.

'No, we're going to drive around and find a nice campground for when mummy comes.'

But first we had a swim. A man, his two young daughters and a thousand horseflies were at the pool.

'Very wise to keep your hat on,' said the man. (I had only brought my panama to freshen it in the water.) 'These darn things are mean.'

Charlie stared at the younger daughter. Glancing myself, I guessed she was about eleven and had Down's Syndrome. She dipped her head into the water then howled.

'Why is she crying?' asked Charlie. 'She's a big girl – she shouldn't cry like that.'

'Come on – swim.'

'But why is she crying? Big girls shouldn't cry like that.'

'Charlie – be quiet.'

'It's OK,' said the father. 'You see, Charlie, she's a special girl. She's a bit different from other children and when she does some things – like putting her face in water – she gets upset. But that's 'cause she's special. She is just different from other kids.'

'What's her name?'

'You ask her Charlie,' urged the father.

'What's your name?'

'Melissa,' said the girl.

'Do you want to come in the shallow end, Melissa? If you come with me, you won't get your head wet.' This was rich coming from a boy who couldn't even swim and often screamed himself when he got his face wet. But I was touched. He played with Melissa until we went for lunch.

Cleaning his teeth that evening, Charlie dropped his toothbrush in the toilet. Things were rather cramped in the RV bathroom.

So, next morning we all had a *campground* shower. As the sun was strong, and as it took so long to dry and dress both boys in the small, wet cubicle, I helped Charlie with his clothes but let Nicolai stroll back, naked, to the RV.

'Sir!' yelled the manager, stopping his small electric cart. (We had met earlier when I checked in.) 'Will you please quit that immediately!'

'What?' I said bemused.

'Will you put a towel or *something* on that child now...'

'Sorry?'

'Your son, sir – cover him up.'

'Eh?'

56

'I said cover him up... Look, that kind of thing may be OK in *your* country but we don't like it here in the United States. At least, I don't. Now please kindly cover up that child.' The man was almost trembling with fury.

'OK,' I said quietly. 'But he's only three years old.'

'I'm sorry, sir – but we just can't have naked people walking round this place.'

I wrapped a towel round Nicolai and carried him back to the RV.

We left that campground, having decided that the best one for Khelga would be Capital KOA, near Baltimore in Maryland. It offered a variety of organised kids' activities as well as a Washington shuttle. I made a reservation, drove back to Fredericksburg and next day we met Khelga at Dulles Airport.

Emerging from the customs hall, she was in a mighty Russian rage. She'd been up late packing the night before and now the airline had lost her luggage. And, as a city girl who's proud to have grown up in Central Moscow (and gets nervous going west over the Hammersmith Flyover), she wasn't looking forward to being stuck in a motorhome in the Maryland countryside for a week. 'How much would it cost to fly to New York?' she asked within only seconds of meeting us. 'We could go and stay with Anastasia...' (a Russian friend and fellow emigrée).

She settled for a drive through Washington DC (it was great having a car – I could keep up with traffic, reverse, and go through low tunnels without worry), then we spent the evening in Fredericksburg.

Next day I returned the rental car and drove the RV to the KOA in Baltimore.

I wasn't looking forward to travelling to Athens. But I had no choice. My taxi for BWI Airport arrived (Baltimore-Washington International – I was flying from there to New York). I kissed everyone goodbye and got in the taxi. Then Nicolai started crying, Charlie followed, Khelga became emotional and even Julia gave a teutonic sniff. I got out of the taxi, kissed them all goodbye again, and got in the taxi for the second time. 'Don't go,' cried Nicolai. 'I'm not going to let you...'

'You're *not* going,' said Charlie. 'I won't let you either.'

My upper lip quivered. I was tempted to stay. Then Khelga said: 'Go.' So I went.

57

15 Baltimore

I returned from Athens a week later. I took a taxi from the airport to the campground and casually strolled to the RV. The two Huffy bicycles were parked outside but the doors of the vehicle were locked. I dropped my suitcases and walked to the playground.

There I found everyone. But they were all subdued. Nicolai had been ill for almost the entire week (so they had not visited Washington) and as he had developed a horrific fever the day before, Khelga had taken him to hospital. He'd been released that morning – with antibiotics and a bill for two hundred and fifty dollars. Luckily we all had insurance. More importantly, Nicolai was feeling better. His eyes were puffy but his fever had gone.

Not daring to risk excursions we spent two more days on the campground. Then, on Khelga's last, we visited Baltimore.

'It's the asshole of America,' a New York friend had told me years before. (I was chasing a girl in Florida at the time and had a rival from Baltimore.) Naturally, the comment had coloured my impressions of the city. But as I now discovered, it wasn't an 'asshole' at all.

Baltimore is located on the western side of Chesapeke Bay, a shellfish-rich estuary which once ruled the Maryland economy. Crabs were caught and tobacco was grown on the eastern side. Baltimore had factories and a thriving port.

The port declined (and when my friend was rude about it, the wharves were rotting and the warehouses derelict), but today the Inner Harbor is revitalised. It has numerous attractions (including a collection of US naval ships – among them the navy's first, an eighteenth-century Baltimore-built frigate), bustling cafés and restaurants and the area swarms with people day and night.

The city also has some fine museums (covering everything from fine arts to black history to urban regeneration), but the biggest attraction is the National Aquarium, located (inevitably) on the Inner Harbour.

The National Aquarium makes Britain's Sealife Centres (and the

London Aquarium) look like goldfish bowls. It's vast (with a rainforest on the roof) and on national holidays rivals Disney World as America's most popular attraction. It certainly helped Nicolai feel better. His favourite creatures were the sharks. And the swimming homo sapiens. To the kids' delight two divers in a tank (serving the fish food) waved to us as we passed. Nicolai tapped the glass. A diver tapped back. My lad quivered with joy.

The emphasis at the National Aquarium is on education. Charlie found the dolphin show highly thought-provoking. A trainer explained that dolphins are mammals — born live and not hatched from eggs. 'Was I hatched from an egg, mummy?' he asked.

'No, darling,' said Khelga. 'Humans are mammals.'

'So are you a mammal, mummy?'

'Yes I am, Charlie.'

We could have happily spent a week in Baltimore. But we only had one day. And as downtown driving was challenging and RV parking expensive (twenty-four dollars as we occupied four spaces) I didn't feel like driving back. We finished our visit cracking crabs in Little Italy (Baltimore oozes seafood restaurants), another restored area adjacent to the Inner Harbour.

The following afternoon I drove Khelga to Washington Dulles Airport. Stupidly, I'd failed to appreciate that as it was Wednesday 2 July squillions of cars would be clogging up Washington as they left for a long holiday weekend. I'd allowed two hours but we spent much of that time grid-locked on the Capital Beltway. Then, as we finally turned off for the airport, the CHECK ENGINE sign started flashing.

However, eventually we arrived. Khelga was forty minutes from departure. 'No worries,' I said, cheerily. She leapt out and ran like a champion to the check-in desk. With a child in each arm I followed like a dishevelled earth-papa. Julia stayed behind to fend off traffic police. Ten minutes later we chaps returned, tears in our eyes. But half an hour later, Nicolai was sleeping and Charlie was about to get some trainers. The prospect put a smile on his face. I pulled into a mall, entered a shoe store and bought him some fifty dollar Nikes. He strolled out of the shops a happy chap.

16 Fourth of July in Washington DC

At Front Royal KOA, Virginia, we met the Pate family from Florida – Dwight and Becky, parents of Lauren, five, Christina, ten, and Dwight Junior ('DJ'), eight. Dwight Senior was a dentist. Becky was a housewife and amateur tennis champion (she also looked after Dwight's office). Their RV was a thirty-three-foot, 1989 model for which they had paid twenty-four thousand dollars in 1996. 'Cheaper than one of our cars,' informed Becky.

Soon we were discussing politics, dentistry and RVs. 'Ours does seven to the gallon which is terrible for a car but great for a home,' said Dwight. 'Now, I guess I'm what you'd call a conservative – I think Ronald Reagan was the best president this country's ever had...You know, there are three major causes of tooth decay in children – genetic, poor diet and bad brushing.'

Front Royal is in the northern part of the Shenandoah Valley and at the beginning of Skyline Drive, a stunningly beautiful scenic highway which runs along the top of the Blue Ridge Mountains. To the south is Shenandoah National Park, a wild area of forests, ravines and waterfalls, 'created' during the Great Depression when hundreds of farms were bought up by the government and the land was left to revert to its natural state.

Because of its fertility and strategic importance, the Shenandoah Valley was a much-fought-over Civil War battleground. It changed hands seventy times at the cost of a hundred thousand dead and maimed. But as well as battlefields, the northern Shenandoah Valley is home to several underground limestone caverns. Dwight drove us to one in his rented people mover. Like many things in America, the cavern was vast (but, unlike Chislehurst Caves in Kent, couldn't boast human residents during World War II, or a Hendrix concert in the 1960s).

That evening (after phoning Cruise America about the CHECK ENGINE sign – they said it was probably a routine reminder to look under the 'hood') I went to the Pates' barbecue. Julia and the kids slept while I slipped out with a six-pack. But I was stopped by a member of the campground staff. 'Sir,' she said, 'you just can't do that.'

'What?' I wondered. 'I'm fully dressed and my kids are in bed...'

'You can't walk around with alcohol like that.'

She explained that alcohol had to be carried in a cover. 'It might seem ridiculous but that's the law. Come over to the shop — I'll give you a bag.' So I accompanied her to the shop, she gave me a paper carrier and I continued the thirty-second walk to the Pates' RV.

Dwight then served the best barbecued steaks I've ever tasted. 'How do you barbecue so brilliantly?' I asked.

'No secret, Matt. Just use natural wood, get the coals burning real red hot, then simply grill the meat, letting the juices drip on to the wood. They evaporate right back into the steak to give it that great smoky flavour.'

The first course was followed by smores. The family couldn't believe I'd never tried them. Dwight took a marshmallow, melted it on tongs above the fire, then sandwiched it between biscuits with Hershey's chocolate. 'There you go Matt — your first Hershey's smore. So-called 'cause you'll want s'more...'

For the Fourth of July we went into Washington DC. Dwight Junior banged on the door at five-thirty a.m. to make sure we were up and at six-fifteen we hit the road — the Pates in their people mover, we in our RV. We left the vehicles at Vienna Park and Ride and took the Metro to Union Station. There we had breakfast — bagels, muffins, donuts, juice and coffee — before casually strolling to the White House.

It wasn't yet nine a.m. but a long queue had already formed outside. 'Two hours' wait,' informed a cop. 'Fourth of July — free entry today.'

We walked up the Mall where participants were gathering for the Fourth of July parade. A line of mounted cowboys filed past. There were TV crews everywhere. 'Will Slick Willie be making an appearance?' shouted Dwight.

'Nope,' a cop replied.

'Thank the Lord!' said Dwight.

Washington DC was born in 1800, following America's independence from Britain (sealed with the Treaty of Paris) in 1783. It was named after George Washington, a Virginian who led the army and then served as the country's first president. (He died in

1799.) Northern and Southern states wanted the capital on their turf and the hundred square miles, bought from Virginia and Maryland, was a compromise resulting in what President Kennedy later (facetiously) called 'a city of Northern charm and Southern efficiency.'

It was laid out by a Frenchman, Pierre L'Enfant. Most major tourist monuments are located in the north-west quadrant along the Mall — a mile of central parkland which stretches from the Capitol to the Potomac River.

In the grounds of the Washington Monument, half-way along the Mall, a theatre was rigged up for a concert. 'Who's playing?' asked Dwight. 'Anyone famous?

'Junior Brown. And I saw Kenny Rogers somewhere,' replied a technician.

After walking in the heat the kids were flagging. We stopped to buy drinks from a stall then, as I carried Nicolai, Dwight carried Lauren and Becky pushed Charlie in Lauren's buggy, we filed past the Vietnam Memorial Wall. 'What's this about, mama?' asked DJ.

'These are the names of men who died serving our country,' replied Becky. (Nearly sixty thousand names are carved on it.)

Dwight made a rubbing (with a free pencil and paper from a kiosk) of the name of a friend's father who had been a MIA (missing in action). We then climbed steps to the Lincoln Memorial where I took a picture of Charlie and Nicolai in front of the enormous white sculpture. I pressed the shutter as they started fighting. The great man stared down from his throne.

Unfortunately we lost the Pates. All the children had wanted to visit the Natural History Museum so we took two taxis and agreed to meet by the gates. But our driver, who barely spoke English, mistakenly deposited us outside the Air and Space Museum (and we didn't realise until too late).

We attempted to walk to the Natural History but, as the kids couldn't walk a block more, settled for the Air and Space.

It's easy to see why this is the world's most popular museum. As you walk in, three fantastic sights confront you — Charles Lindbergh's *Spirit of St Lewis*, the plane in which he made the first solo non-stop Atlantic crossing in 1927; the command module of Apollo 11, which carried Neil Armstrong and his team to the moon in 1969; and a small chip of dark green moon rock.

'That didn't come from the moon,' said Charlie after we'd queued up to see it.

'I promise it did.'

'You're joking,' he replied. 'I don't believe you.'

The museum is vast. In every direction you're drawn to planes, rockets and bits of amazing machinery.

We zipped around the recreated hangar deck of an aircraft carrier, played on a flight simulator (Nicolai and Charlie 'crashed and burnt'), and saw the Wright Brothers 1903 Flyer and the partly restored fuselage of the *Enola Gay*, the plane that dropped the first atom bomb on Hiroshima in 1945 (and the museum's most controversial exhibit). As we left we passed under two inter-continental ballistic missiles (an American Pershing and a Russian SS-20). 'If the Cold War hadn't ended,' I reflected, 'I might not be here with my boys.'

Back at Vienna Park and Ride I left a note on the Pates' people mover (and three months later received a letter packed with photos) and started our drive south to the Smokies then Nashville.

17 Virginia

Half a mile from Shenandoah Park I filled up at a 'Last Gas Before The Park' station (at one thirty-three a gallon — it was the most expensive so far). Then we hit Skyline Drive. The mountainous scenery was glorious ('Like the south of Germany,' said Julia) but the daylight soon started fading. We would be driving along the famous scenic highway in darkness.

After ninety minutes we stopped at a viewing site. It was almost dark. Other cars joined us. Drivers and passengers sat on a wall. Showers of light filled the sky. These were the Fourth of July fireworks over Washington. We drove for three more hours and spent the night at Lexington.

Lexington is full of Civil War memorials. The Confederate General Robert E. Lee is buried in the crypt of the Lee Chapel — his horse is buried outside. And the military museum of the Virginia Military Institute explains the story of the only university in US history to have sent all its students into a single battle.

On US11 we stopped at an ancient-looking grocery store, advertising 'Fresh Local Produce'. 'Those are actually Californian,' the shopkeeper muttered apologetically, as I put some apples in a bag. 'But they're good... Real good. It's too early for local Virginia apples.' I picked up some peaches. 'Same goes for peaches... But they're real good too.' We took the fruit, a honeycomb, and some ham. 'Now, that's Virginia-cured, I can assure you.'

He rang up the items on an ancient cash-register. 'Had it since 1954,' he said proudly. 'And it's great for business.' Then he complained about Wallmart which made life difficult for traders like him. 'But in a way, you know, those stores do me a favour too. They make people want to shop the old-fashioned way.' He showed us his scales which also dated from the 1950s. 'These are pretty good for business, too.'

He asked about our trip and when I told him where we'd started he smiled. 'Orlando, eh?' he reflected, nostalgically. 'Went there for my honeymoon in 1948. It was beautiful then – I remember the orange blossom. There was no man-made stuff. But I went back years later and it was all artificial.'

His name was Carlton Leynes. I introduced myself and said we were heading towards the Smokies.

'You're going to the Smokies? Wow!' he said, excitedly. 'Well, y'all look out for those bears.'

Charlie looked tense. 'Did he say bears? Daddy, let's not go to the Smokies.'

Nicolai smirked. 'A bear's going to eat you.'

'Don't be ridiculous,' I said. 'We'll stay in our RV.'

'Will he eat our RV?'

'Definitely not. Bears can't bite through metal.'

'But it's not all metal, daddy. Some of it's plastic.'

Carlton said farewell and wished us luck. Then he added mischievously: 'And remember – look out for those bears.' Charlie scampered into the RV.

Once out of Shenandoah National Park, Skyline Drive becomes the Blue Ridge Parkway. This winds along the crests of the Southern Appalachian Mountains for four hundred and sixty-nine miles until it reaches the Great Smoky Mountains National Park. We sampled a stretch down to Roanoke. We were three thousand plus feet high. The views were superb. Giant trees and wild flowers were everywhere. If I hadn't had the kids I'd have dumped the RV and hiked.

In Roanoke I got on to Interstate 81. Unfortunately, the part near the Tennessee border was closed for repair. Signs diverted me. Dusk began to fall. Julia and the kids slept soundly (probably just as well because at one point we ended up in North Carolina – I didn't have a clue where I was going). Then the RV got damaged again. A truck thundered towards me as I crossed a narrow bridge. Refusing to decelerate, it forced me to one side and I scraped a luggage panel on the bridge wall. The clash made a hideous scraping sound. Julia awoke with a start. 'What was that?' she asked. I stopped and examined what I expected would be a mess. Luckily the paintwork was only slightly scratched and two panel locks rather bent.

We ended up in Newport, Tennessee. I pulled in at a gas station on a snaking, country road.

'How mu-choo gear-t?' asked the cashier.

'Sorry?' I said.

'How much gas choo buy?'

'About twenty bucks' worth, I think.'

'That'll do.'

'That'll do? Don't you have a computer here?'

'Broken,' replied the cashier, unconcerned.

Outside a cop was talking to a good ole boy in a stained vest and cap who intermittently chewed and spat. I asked the cop if he knew of a nearby campground. 'Hold on,' he said and drifted away. He returned with some sweets, offered me the packet and popped one into his mouth. Then he sucked slowly and reflected.

'So do you know where a *campground* is?' I prompted. He popped another sweet into his mouth and started thinking again. The ole boy stayed silent, occasionally spitting. After what seemed like eternity, the cop said: 'Wait...I'll go get a map.'

He walked over to his patrol car, took one out, carefully sketched a route on it, then gave the map to me. 'Thanks,' I said briskly and started my engine.

'Say...' he drawled. 'Would y'all be from Australia?'

'England,' I said.

'That so?' replied the cop. 'Well, I'll be darned.'

I hastily said farewell, continued straight, then turned round in a Wallmart parking-lot. This was *the* place for Newport youth. Cars full of kids raced around it. 'Welcome to Newport,' howled an obviously drunk girl, leaning out of a passenger window. Half a dozen cars sped off. 'Idiots!' I said, sounding extremely middle-aged. 'Spending Saturday night in a Wallmart parking-lot.'

'Well, we do similar things in Germany,' said Julia. 'But we drive to different McDonald's...'

We arrived at the campground at one a.m. Julia showered and retired. I fried a steak and washed it down with a Budweiser. Then I went to bed.

'Good-morning, daddy. Did you have a nice dream?' It was five-thirty a.m. and Charlie was wrenching open my eyelids.

Nicolai soon joined him. 'Daddy, there's a spot on my *popka*.' (Russian for bottom — a common word at home.) A bug had bitten him. I scratched my own bottom — I'd been bitten too.

18 The Smoky Mountains

As I rarely had more than fifty dollars in my pocket I was dependent upon my credit cards. These had been used heavily during previous weeks so I decided to check on my finances.

'Your balance is two thousand two hundred and twenty-six pounds and forty-two pence,' said the twenty-four-hour service line assistant. It was three a.m. in Britain. 'That's four hundred and seventy-six pounds and forty-two pence over your credit limit.'

'Well, a cheque for five hundred is in the post. Can I increase my limit?'

'No problem, sir. How much would you like?'

The next call was almost as straightforward. The only problem was the line. 'I'm sorry I can hardly hear you,' I bawled. 'I'm ringing from America, from a payphone on a campground near some toilets, so you'll have to shout a bit too...' The assistant raised her voice and told me my balance. I promised a cheque. Then she increased my credit limit.

'Nice work,' I thought. It was good to be flush again.

Later I phoned Khelga at work and asked her to send some of the pre-signed cheques I'd left. I told her we were in the Smokies; that Nicolai was better; that we'd been into Washington; that it was hot; that Nicolai had a bite on his bottom; that I had one too...' And she told me to go. All phone calls are recorded in her office (in case the bank's transactions ever need to be checked) and she was worried her boss might hear some unsavoury domestic details.

It was a shame to put the phone down because I had loads of talking time. Telephone cards on this trip were a godsend. When I first went to America you needed a bucketful of quarters to call transatlantic from a payphone. You'd ring the operator, she would connect your call, you'd hear the person answer and the operator would say dramatically: 'Hello, this is the United States... Caller, please put in seven dollars, fifty cents now...' You fed in thirty quarters while the other party patiently hung on. The operator would then say: 'Go ahead, caller. You have three minutes.' You would talk. Time would fly and the moment you'd used your allotted time, an automatic voice requested more cash. But you'd continue talking until you were cut off. You'd then put the phone down. It would ring back and the automatic voice would say: 'Please put in seven dollars and fifty cents now...' At this point you'd leave the receiver dangling and run away (and the poor folks you'd been calling – usually your parents – would probably be billed for the transatlantic call).

With phonecards you buy pre-paid time. You dial an access line, punch in a PIN and call your number (for Britain that can total forty digits). Virgin Atlantic had sold American phonecards but during my Athens flights I had found companies in airline magazines offering incredibly cheap deals. I'd bought some time and got my transatlantic calls down to just a few pence a minute. The only thing to watch was that these bargain companies automatically redebited your credit card as soon as your prepaid time ran low.

Charlie's Smokies bear-fear was unfounded. The only bears we saw were those which had seen the taxidermist. They were in glass cases in Visitors' Centers. But we did see vast quantities of cars. It was nose to bumper all the way through the Great Smoky Mountains National Park. And as for the towns – Pigeon Forge, Gatlinburg, Cherokee – I've never seen such tacky tourist hangouts – full of motels, fast-food places, souvenir stores, fairgrounds, factory outlets and even waxwork museums!

But the Smokies themselves are beautiful. They take their name from a bluish haze (the condensation of vapours from the thick vegetation) which also hangs above the Blue Ridge Mountains. And despite human invasions they're home to fifteen hundred different types of plants and flowers, as well as various wild animals – hogs, deer, wild turkeys, wolves and, of course, bears among them. The best way to see the land is to hike – there are marked trails in the park – although we took a bus tour from Gatlinburg.

19 Chatanooga, Tennessee

We spent the night in Cherokee. This was a strange place, full of dedicated Cherokee buildings – the Cherokee Youth Camp; the Cherokee School; the Cherokee Playground; the Cherokee First Church of God... A funfair was at the beginning of town – at the end of a tunnel through a mountain to the National Park. The rides were manned by blank-faced Cherokee youths who'd obviously had a frenzied previous day working the Fourth of July holiday. Now, all was quiet and they were bored.

The KOA was huge – the biggest since Myrtle Beach. Greeters were at the entrance. 'Good-afternoon,' said one with a familiar accent.

'Good-afternoon.' Her name badge said 'Svetlana'.

I checked in. The reception was like a United Nations youth branch. Half the staff were European. A Swedish girl told me they were all on exchange programmes. A Polish girl took my registration. Meanwhile a couple of bad-tempered campers demanded to speak to an American.

After supper the boys were grouchy. We now had only two days before Julia flew home. Charlie got emotional when he realised she was leaving. 'I want to live in Germany,' he sobbed.

But soon they were sleeping and while the boys recharged their batteries I had a beer with our neighbour. His name was Walt and he was from Atlanta. His motorhome was small but, as he boasted, he worked for Delta Airlines so he normally *flew* off on vacation. 'That's the benefit of working for an airline. I can go anywhere in the whole damn world for ten per cent of the standard fare.'

'That's a *great* benefit,' I said. 'So where in the world have you been?'

'What? Like different countries?'

'Yeh.'

Walt hesitated before telling me. 'Nowhere...'

'Nowhere?'

'Nope. Not different countries, anyroad. America's so damn beautiful, I don't need to travel the world. I ain't even got myself a passport. There's so much of the United States to see.'

Once the kids were awake I got the urge to press on further. I unhooked the RV and drove for three hours until we arrived at a campground just outside Chatanooga.

I was woken at six a.m. by Nicolai on my bunk. 'OK,' I said. 'You can stay here if you scratch my back,' This was now our ongoing deal. (Just as it had been with my father and me when I was small.) As usual Nicolai's efforts were useless. 'I know!' I exclaimed, inspired. 'Why don't we buy daddy a backscratcher?'

The campground shop didn't stock them but the concept fascinated the kids. 'How will it work?' asked Charlie. 'Will it have batteries? Does a special hand scratch your back?' I explained it was a big plastic fork.

The city of Chatanooga was made famous by Glenn Miller's *Chatanooga Choo-Choo* (the name given by the local paper to the first passenger train to arrive from Cincinatti in 1880). But it was actually the last capital of the Cherokee nation. In the 1830s, fourteen thousand Cherokee were forcibly removed (and thousands died) on an ethnic-cleansing trek to Oklahoma. Known as the 'Trail of Tears', it explained the Native American emphasis in Cherokee.

The Chatanooga Regional History Museum has a display on the Cherokee but the town's most popular tourist draws are its aquarium, the 'largest freshwater aquarium in the world', and various railway attractions.

At Grand Junction (home of the Tennessee Valley Railroad Museum) the kids were enthralled by the locos collection. But when a real, live, working train arrived at the platform both stood in awe, mesmerised. For Nicolai, this was no mere machine but a great, hissing, steaming, whistling, monster. The train came to a halt. Nicolai halted too. The engine was feet from us – Charlie and I approached it. But Nicolai, usually fearless, hung back. The driver gave a blast on its deafening whistle. Nicolai jumped. He wouldn't go near the snorting head. We boarded a carriage and the train left for East Chatanooga.

Our tickets were collected by a high-school teacher called Bruce. Seeing him dressed in turn-of-the-century US railwayman's gear, I would never have guessed that he wasn't a realrail road man. 'We're all volunteers, although the driver's a former pro...' he announced over the train's PA system. Then he gave a technical description of the engine – 'Not bad for a liberal-arts graduate.'

At East Chatanooga the engine was turned around on a eighty-foot-long turntable. Charlie was entranced. 'That's what happened to James in *Thomas the Tank Engine*,' he gushed. 'And he got dizzy on his turntable.' Bruce then led us to the engine shed where we saw cranes and sunken track, still used for steam-train repairs.

Back at Grand Junction Charlie and Nicolai were drawn to the hissing engine. The driver poked his head out and spoke. His name was Bert and he told us he'd spent forty-three years working on the Louisville (Kentucky) to Nashville (Tennessee) line.

To Charlie's joy he invited us into the cab. I lifted each boy up and the Casey Jones figure grabbed them in his huge, gauntlet-clad hands. I followed. Nicolai was apprehensive, Charlie fascinated. To his delight, Bert let him try the driver's seat. Charlie asked Bert if he knew Thomas. 'I beg your pardon?' said the driver.

'You know,' said Charlie, 'Thomas the Tank Engine – the train with the face.'

'Oh, Thomas,' said Bert. 'The British steam engine... No, I don't know him. But I've got a British pen pal – he's a railway enthusiast. And some day I'll visit the York Railway Museum.' Our conversation ended when other parents gathered, offering up their own kids, like sacrifices, to the river. 'Sorry, folks,' he said. 'We gotta go.'

I made lunch in the Grand Junction parking-lot and drove to the town's former railroad terminal, now a hotel (the Chattanooga Choo-Choo Holiday Inn) which offers rooms in restored sleeper cars. The hotel also houses one of the largest model railways in the world. We had a look. It beat the Brio at home (the wooden model railways many toddlers have) then set off for Nashville to meet America.

20 Nashville and Memphis

My first impressions of Nashville came on the city outskirts. THE BIGGEST BIBLE STORE IN THE WORLD said a billboard on the roof of a warehouse-shop. THOUSANDS OF BIBLES PERMANENTLY IN STOCK – MANY AT 50% DISCOUNT. I drove another half-mile then saw another billboard: THE BIGGEST ADULT BOOKSTORE IN AMERICA – HUNDREDS OF TITLES AT GREATLY REDUCED PRICES.

We were now on Central Time – one hour behind Chatanooga. It was six p.m. and Nashville rush-hour traffic was horrendous – faster and more terrifying than anything around Washington. To make matters worse we couldn't even find the airport turning. Julia's usually masterful navigational skills couldn't identify the road on the map. Suddenly I saw a sign and swerved to leave the Interstate. Behind me I heard a screech of tyres. A car flew past, its driver mouthing insults while thrashing a finger up and down. 'Silly man,' said Julia, like a sensible aunt. 'He was far too close.'

We arrived at the airport and I parked on the roof of the short-term lot.

America looked dazed after her two-flights trip. The kids and I greeted her and we introduced Julia.

'So welcome to Nashville,' said the check-in woman at Opryland KOA. 'You're on Tex Ritter Drive. Next to Tammy Wynette Lane.'

I am not a country-music fan. Nor was America. Nor was Julia. This is a drawback in Nashville.

The city's most famous family attraction draw is Opryland, a country-music-theme park built around the studios of *The Grand Ole Opry*, America's longest running radio show (it originally specialised in showcasing new performers, and in 1954 a young man called Presley didn't pass the audition – they told him to stick to truck-driving). We also did the Country Music Hall of Fame, a voyeur's heaven, packed with stars' possessions – like a pair of Jim Reeves' shoes, Elvis's gold Cadillac, Webb Pieke's dollar-bill-plastered car, Hank Williams's stage outfit, Patsy Cline's wig and, less edifying, the battered lighter that was found at the scene of the air crash that killed her.

But bars and clubs were out. And so were Nashville's endless, really tacky, attractions — horrid little places where you pay to gawp at totally insignificant former possessions of tirelessly exploited country singers. We weren't interested in free family line-dance sessions in the Wild Horse Saloon, nor in producing our own family version of some country hit in the You're The Star recording studio. But the boys loved the campground — it had a good pool, there were hundreds of kids, and free performances were staged every night.

One day we cruised around town. Nashville has a big non-country side — it's a major financial centre (known as the 'Wall Street of the South') and also a place of learning for trainee preachers (often tagged the 'Protestant Vatican'). We drove past the Parthenon (Nashville's very own replica of the Greek original — yet another Nashville tag is the 'Athens of the South') and the Museum of Beverage Containers (filled with thirty-six thousand cans, the world's largest collection — whoopee!). We ended up, inevitably, at the Nashville Toy Museum.

Because we were British the owner didn't charge us admission. That was a smart move because once they'd seen his ancient toys the boys demanded some modern ones from his shop. Charlie presented his case for a treat: 'It's not fair, daddy. You never buy us anything. You always only want us to look...'

He was right. I take the boys to Hamleys frequently. It's not just Britain's finest toyshop but also a good free trip out. Great toys are everywhere and they've spent many happy hours, playing with displays. But you can't *buy* them a toy every time.

Here though, relaxed in the knowledge of newly raised credit card limits, I splashed out on some glove puppets. The boys were very appreciative.

Julia's flight day arrived fast. Before the airport we went to an outlet mall. She bought some jeans. I needed new trainers — mine were seriously stinky.

The assistant fetched a range. 'Those are definitely best, sir...' he said when I tried the giant pair. 'The thirteens really do fit you best.'

'But that's impossible...' . 'Well, Adidas come up small, sir. They're probably only a twelve in other makes.'

'You honestly think so?'

'I do...' So I took them. When I entered the RV, proudly wearing my new purchase, the two girls became hysterical with giggles.

'Look!' shrieked Julia, placing a foot next to mine. 'They're so huge and white!' I decided to rough them up a bit (the trainers not the girls). To splash them in a puddle the moment I found one (which, with the relentless heat, now probably meant waiting till we were back in Britain). To rub in some dirt, take off that shine and destroy the horrible prospect of sporting gleaming, goofy, size thirteen white trainers.

Arriving at the airport, we all became subdued. But then Julia, who already had a punishing schedule ahead of her (Nashville–Chicago–Heathrow–Cologne), learnt that British Airways were on strike and that, after arriving in London (with American Airlines), she would be given a Lufthansa stand-by but first have to take a bus from Heathrow to Gatwick.

'You are not serious...' she yelped, John McEnroe-style. 'Please tell me now, you're not serious...'

'I'm afraid it's true,' said the check-in woman, limply.

'But this is appalling... Why did I not book in the first place with Lufthansa? Typical disorganised British company...!' We accompanied a spluttering Julia to her plane (non-flyers can go right to the gate in America), the poignancy of the moment tarnished by her fury. But it was sad to say goodbye. She had been a great help and friend. As we left the terminal Charlie started crying. I started sniffling. Nicolai demanded a Coke.

'OK,' I said to America when we reached the RV. 'Can you direct me out of this space?'

'Well, actually...' she admitted. 'I failed my driving test only last week. But I'll do my best.' It wasn't a big challenge. We were parked on the roof again and there was only one car up there.

'How are we doing?' I asked, leaning out of the window as I started to reverse.

'Fine,' she said, motioning uncertainly with her hands.

'Can I keep going?'

'Yes...'

'More?'

'Yes...'

'More?'

'Yes...'

'OK?'

'Yes...'

'Still OK?'

'Yes...'

'OK?'

'Yes...' BANG! SCRATCH... We had hit a parking-lot bollard.

'Sorry,' said America. 'I wasn't watching that side...'

'Never mind,' I said, feeling stupid to have tried this. 'What are you like at map-reading?'

'Well, to be honest, whenever I go anywhere with my friends by car, I'm usually the one who doesn't pay attention to the route. I tell the stories and jokes and things...'

'Right...' I said. 'Well, here's the atlas. We're in Tennessee...'

Our next campground was just north of Nashville. The receptionist was on the phone. 'I can't talk now, Billy, I'm extremely busy...' She put down the phone to check us in. 'Choose whatever site you like, sir, 'cos we're not busy at all...'

But by early evening there was more activity. And Charlie went missing. I turned my attention for thirty little seconds and the boy completely disappeared. Mercifully, he was soon returned by a camper.

'Mr Collins?' the man asked. He was holding Charlie's hand.

'Oh, thank God, you've got him! Did Charlie tell you my name?'

'Sure did. And he gave me a good description of you...'

'What did he say?'

'Well... He said his dad was bald, not very tall and had big feet. So I guessed you must be him...'

'Thanks...'

'No problem. Take it easy. And don't you wander off again, Charlie.'

Our final stop in Nashville was for an oil change at Jiffy Lube. Cruise America renters have to change it every three thousand miles – the company reimburses the cost. The kids were fascinated to watch so many hands go over the exhaust, tyres and engine. After being assured that everything was fine (and that the CHECK ENGINE was a routine reminder and *probably* nothing to worry about) we set off for Memphis.

Memphis was marvellous. Even the drive was exciting. At an Interstate Rest Area, we saw two manacled men, their hands and feet chained, being lead from the rest rooms to a van. They were accompanied by two plain-clothes cops (the guns and handcuffs were a giveaway). Charlie and Nicolai tried to follow the poor prisoners.

'Have they been arrested?' asked Charlie.

'Yes,' I said quietly. And led the boys off to a drinks machine.

'But why have they been arrested?'

The idea of arrest intrigued him because, perhaps wrongly, I'd said a few times that we could get arrested if we misbehaved — that was why they had to sit properly at the table when we were driving, why I couldn't go fast, and why they must never open the RV door when we were moving....

'We won't be arrested, will we daddy?'

'Definitely not, Charlie. We won't be naughty...' The threat of being manacled did seem excessive.

In Memphis another prisoner came to mind. There was a radio news story about a possible retrial for James Earl Ray. He'd been convicted of Martin Luther King's murder downtown thirty-one years before and DNA tests on bullets had produced some new evidence in his favour. (Unfortunately, Ray died months later.) Immediately after the news, the station played an Elvis song. I'd already told the boys about the King and that we were going to see his house. 'Listen, boys,' I said. 'This is an Elvis Presley song...'

Charlie was mystified. 'But how can Elvis sing if he's dead?'

21 The King of Rock 'n' Roll

Graceland KOA is next to Graceland itself on Elvis Presley Boulevard. The sites border the Graceland parking-lot. When Elvis bought his eleven-bedroomed home here in 1957, EP Boulevard had been a high-class area. Now it's a neon-lit strip of motels, gas stations, fast-food outlets and souvenir shops. Every establishment offers some Elvis connection. The Days Inn had a sign saying 'Free Elvis Movie In Every Room'. The campground named its lanes after songs. 'You're on Blue Suede Lane,' said the platinum blonde grand-mother at the registration counter. 'Go up Love Me Tender Boulevard, make a left on Heartbreak Hotel Lane, go past Hound Dog Way, past All Shook Up and Don't Be Cruel Lanes and you're the last on the left.'

'Thank you,' I said, confused.

The kids were amused by the goods on sale. Most campgrounds stock some food and drink and numerous cheap plastic toys. But this store was stuffed with souvenirs. 'Look,' said Charlie, triumphantly. 'An Elvis Presley backscratcher!' He held aloft a large plastic fork. I *had* to buy it. We skipped to the RV. I should have bought two – the boys started fighting over who was going to have the privilege of scratching my back.

But that novelty soon wore off. So, with great excitement, it was through the gate to Graceland.

I must admit I've never been a huge Elvis fan. I only became aware of him properly once he'd reached his overweight, green-rhinestone-sequinned cat-suit phase. But I did learn his most famous number during my first year at Hampton Grammar School. The words weren't original but they appealed to a twelve-year-old. Forgive me while I briefly reminisce:

> Going to a party at the county jail,
> Caught my bollocks on a rusty nail;
> When I came home, had a terrible shock,
> Only one ball and half a cock.
> Let's rock...
> Ooh ooh ooh – let's rock...

It wasn't quite the thing to be singing as we entered the King's house. But I didn't know the real words. (And I didn't even know the rest of the schoolboy version – something like: 'Asked my mama what to do; She said stick it together, son, with Bostick glue; Ooh ooh ooh – let's rock...') But the tune helped me get into the mood. And, anyhow, the visit converted me.

What a man, Presley was. A softly spoken, courteous revolutionary who at first didn't seem to realise his huge effect. One of the world's richest men with some of the world's simplest tastes. ('I don't know much about art but I can admire a good house job...') I'm not certain what overall impression the Graceland tour had on the kids (you're shuffled round the 1970s interiors, although upstairs is out of bounds) but they enjoyed it. The display which made the biggest impact was the television, complete with bullet-holed screen, (on display in the *Sincerely Elvis* museum) that Elvis had fired at in anger (apparently during a ball game). That sparked conversations for days. 'Elvis was naughty to fire at his television. He could have been arrested,' said Charlie.

They were fascinated by his firearms – dozens of them. I was impressed by his Trophy Room (wall-to-wall gold and platinum discs), his record collection (there were albums by Tom Jones and Elton John) and his personal toiletries – the Hai Karate and Brut meant that in the early seventies I had the same aftershave tastes as the King. Tastes my father never shared – he grew up before the days of aftershave *and political correctness*. 'Ugh!' he'd say, as I spruced myself up for the Walton Hop. 'You smell like an Egyptian tram car!' (He was in Cairo during the War.)

After Nicolai had unsuccessfully tried to abseil into Lisa Marie's playground (he shinned up a fence when he spotted a slide and was immediately bawled at by a guard), we, and a long stream of visitors, paid our respects in the Meditation Garden where the Presley family are buried – mom Gladys, dad Vernon, grandma, his stillborn twin Jesse and, of course, Elvis himself. Presley's body was moved there shortly after his death (when it became obvious that keeping it in the local cemetery would pose a security problem). His grave was strewn with flowers – they still arrive daily from fans.

Elvis died on 16 August 1977. We visited on 12 July 1997. I was glad we'd made it before the anniversary. ('It's goin' to be crazy,' the woman on the KOA desk informed me later. 'I been fully booked for a year...')

We left his grave and boarded his planes, *Houndog II* and the *Lisa Marie* (personally customised with seats in 'Florida Lime and Sunshine Yellow', gold-plated seat belts, rest rooms with twenty-four-carat-gold-flecked sinks, game tables, TVs, quadrophonic stereo, sofas, recliners and a queen-size bed). Then we visited the Elvis Automobile Museum (home to his pink Cadillac and gasoline credit cards). If you don't buy the 'Platinum Tour Package' you pay extra to see each attraction.

After our Presley overdose I debriefed the boys. 'So who was Elvis Presley?'

'A soldier?' asked Charlie (a good enough guess — we'd seen enough guns and uniforms).

'No. Try again...'

'King of Rock and Roll?'

'Well done. And what did he do?'

'He died...'

'Yes, but before he died?'

'He sang...'

'And what did he sing?'

'Rock and roll...'

'Excellent.' This trip was educational after all. Later however, downtown on Beale Street, we spotted a life-size poster of Elvis. 'So boys,' I said: 'Who is that man?'

'Is it John Major?' asked Charlie.

22 Downtown Memphis and the Mippy Lippy

Next morning, after washing in the campground rest rooms (which, in the midst of Memphis tat, had an extremely incongruous print of *Prince George's Favourite Things* by the English artist Sir Edwin Lutyens [1802-1873] hanging above the sinks), we went to the Pyramid, first port of call for 'Titanic — The Exhibition'.

The Pyramid is a thirty-two-storey, three-hundred-and-twenty-one-foot-high stainless-steel events centre (two-thirds the size of the Great Pyramid in Giza — a city, like Memphis, on the delta of a great river) which dominates the waterfront skyline.

Our bags were checked by a team of women who looked sufficiently advanced in years to have been *Titanic* passengers themselves. One was so frail she had trouble lifting up my video camera. 'We're all volunteers,' said a more sprightly member of the corps. 'It's a scheme in Memphis — to give retired folk work in the community.' Other senior ladies gave us some headsets to make the audio tour.

The exhibition — the largest collection of (incredibly well-preserved) artefacts recovered from the ship — was riveting. Even Charlie and Nicolai were absorbed. They both knew the story as I'd told them it months before (in the same way my dad had told me when I was small — although that was decades before the wreck was discovered).

Among the artefacts were chandeliers, diamond necklaces, a steward's jacket, porthole covers, a bronze cherub and two bottles of champagne (with their corks intact). But the most touching exhibit was a pocket watch — lost with the drowned father of a surviving baby girl. And presented to her eight decades later.

As well as telling the tragic story, the exhibition reveals the ship as an Edwardian time capsule and gives a convincing impression of what life was really like on board. Visitors can tour the *Titanic* in virtual reality. One area has a replica of the deck. You look out on to the sea and star-filled sky (simulated with colours and lights). The scene is so amazingly atmospheric that Charlie was wary about going near the edge just in case he fell into the (non-existent) water. The exhibition (currently touring America) naturally raises questions about the morality of disturbing a sea grave but is undeniably captivating.

Some souvenirs in the shop however, were *very* tacky. The 'olde-English' gifts – such as daintily packaged teas and jams – were fine. And even captain's caps with *Titanic* emblazoned on them weren't *so* bad. But '*Titanic*' Christmas-tree decorations?

'Wow!' said a stunned American visitor. 'They'll be making Flight 1-800 captain's hats and decorations next...'

Leaving the RV in the Pyramid parking-lot (and our valuables with the trusty security girls) we took the monorail to Mud Island.

'Is this the Mippi Lippy?' asked Charlie when he saw the river. We did the 'Mississippi Walk' (a replica of the real thing carved into the ground) and ended up at its own 'Gulf of Mexico' complete with swimming pool, playground and artificial beach.

The kids played on the swings, the downtown Memphis skyscape behind them. 'Downriver' was the *Memphis Belle*, a World War II B17 (Flying Fortress) bomber, made famous in the eponymous film. Beside it were two real vets. We spoke to Ross Witherspoon, a former B17 rear gunner who saw active service over Germany and the Balkans.

Ross was wearing a '483rd Bombing Group' baseball hat and belt with matching, 'Flying Fortress – 483rd Bombing Group' buckle. But he was modest about his experiences. 'No, sir, I can't tell you how many hits I got – cos you never knew when enemy planes dived if they were going to come up again...'

After the war, he had been based in Burton Wood near Warrington. 'You been to Blackpool?' he asked, eagerly.

'Of course,' I replied.

'You like it?'

'Yes, it's great...'

'Oh boy, it certainly is... We had some fun there and I was in Blackpool for the first post-war illuminations...'

Ross's service career had then taken him to Margate. 'Wasn't quite such fun...' But he stayed in the airforce and later saw service in

Korea and Vietnam. 'I taught the Vietnamese to fly light aircraft – Cessnas and little things like that...'

The other vet was a former bomber pilot. He was about eighty, stooped and wore a hearing aid but was surrounded by admirers whose questions he lapped up.

'What a great idea,' I thought. 'We should use our own WWII vets like that.' (My dad spent the war in the RAF – though he's often reluctant to talk about his own experiences. 'Did you ever kill a man?' I asked as a kid. 'You don't want to know that,' he'd reply.)

We strolled back along the river walk with a 'Mississippi Guide' called Kent. He showed us round Mud Island's very own concert stadium saying this was a music promoter's dream. 'Because, as it's on an island, only ticket holders get in...' He informed us that Barry Manilow was due to play there soon.

Shortly afterwards, on Beale Street, we came across a throng of Manilow fans, all wearing 'I'm one of Barry's women' badges. One group contained two men (their badges said: 'We love Barry'). 'Well you don't have to be female to like him,' said a guy. 'I've been following Barry for over twenty years...'

He told us they were in town for the Manilow Convention at the Crown Plaza Hotel. 'Will Manilow be there?' I asked.

'Not in person,' the male fan admitted. 'But people from his fan club will be telling us what he's up to...'

He said they were travelling to Nashville for the evening (a round trip of four hundred miles) to see him perform. Then they were going to the Memphis concert before travelling to Birmingham, Alabama where they were going to see him for a third time. 'You see Barry's not a hero,' gushed the guy, madly, 'he's a way of life...'

'Nutcases!' said America, as they walked into the distance.

Beale Street, so-called 'Birthplace of the Blues', and centre of downtown tourist Memphis, was once a black cultural centre. In its heyday before World War II it was home to vaudeville theatres, concert halls, bars, gambling dens, brothels and numerous other attractions. Here the young Elvis found cool suits and musical inspiration.

In the 1960s the area declined (helped, ironically, by the Civil Rights Movement which opened up the rest of Memphis to blacks) but today it's a restored 'historic district' with shops, clubs and cafés bedecked 1920s-style. We peeked in A. Schwab's Dry Goods Store (owned by the same family since 1876, it still stocks voodoo powders and potions) and headed for Sun Studios where Elvis, Jerry Lee Lewis, Johnny Cash and Carl Perkins made their first recordings (under producer Sam Phillips who famously said: 'If I could find a white man with the Negro sound and feel, I could make a billion dollars' — he found his man in Presley). We stopped for a drink in Alfred's bar (where the kids were impressed by the blues singer who could play guitar, mouth-organ and sing — almost simultaneously) before making a discovery which was a hit with the kids.

The Police Museum, on Beale Street, is open twenty-four hours a day and admission is free. It's located in a working police station and has a regular cop at the front desk.

For the second time in Memphis, Charlie and Nicolai were fascinated by a large display of firearms. 'Did Elvis shoot his television with those guns?' asked Charlie. The museum also featured police motorbikes and helmets. Several were British. But the most interesting exhibit for the boys was the traditional cell — a self-contained cage within the station, complete with all-in-one sink/commode. Before leaving the museum I picked up some leaflets produced by the Memphis Police Department.

'DON'T LET YOUR FAMILY GO DOWN THE TUBE,' said one. 'Please use television wisely.' Suggestions followed: 'Set limits on what children can watch. Make homework and a meal with the family a priority. Make one room a TV-free zone... Limit video games to half an hour a day... Use a kitchen timer.'

Outside, a sudden fierce storm had broken out. It was pouring and we were dressed in shorts and T-shirts. A man rushed up to us. 'Umbrella accompaniment, sir? Only a dollar... Keep the kids dry...?'

Further up the street another man ripped open his shirt to reveal a torso-sized, crucifix tattoo. 'Take my picture, sir? Only a dollar... Just a single dollar to take my picture...'

We were running low on food so, having picked up the RV from the Pyramid parking-lot, I drove to a mall only to find the supermarket — Family Dollar — shut. I asked a woman with five kids in a clapped-out people mover where the nearest open grocery store was. 'You want Piggly-Wiggly, honey — it's right behind you on Presley Boulevard...'

I drove to Piggly-Wiggly. It was now nine p.m.; the parking-lot was dark and this area did not look safe. But we desperately needed food, so I asked America if she was OK with the (now sleeping) children while I did a lightning-speed shop. She agreed, so I pulled up close to the store entrance, asked the armed security man at the door to watch our RV, and ran in for a supermarket sweep.

Hovering momentarily by fruit and veg (which during this trip I had often found surprisingly less fresh and tasty than in Britain – I'd come across several out-of-date sell-by stickers) a voice came over the in-store PA: 'Attention, attention – misting is about to take place. Please stand back if you do not wish to get wet. Misting is the process of watering vegetables which keeps them healthy and fresh for you...'

'Yes,' I thought, 'and looking more enticing than they deserve to be...' (And these weren't the only disappointments. The number of additives in American food products was unbelievable – even the label on a bottle of mineral water informed me that it contained 'selected minerals – added for flavour and taste'.)

I filled up my trolley and reached the cashier in five minutes. As I queued, my eyes scanned the lead story of *The Commercial Appeal:* AS MEMPHIS ROBBERIES RISE, MORE WOMEN GET IN THE LINE OF CRIME. The newspaper carried a security-camera picture of 'The Most Wanted Bank Robber in Memphis'. The culprit was female. 'Believed to have robbed three banks in three years...'

I had heard snippets about crime and racial problems in Memphis – on the radio, from other campers and from a local who'd warned me about travelling on local buses. 'You know, you wanna be real careful, sir. Nearly all the passengers are black...'

'So what?' I said. Her eyes almost popped right out of her head.

We tried the buses in Memphis and didn't have a problem. Being British obviously helped but one black kid gave up his seat for Nicolai before he'd even heard us speak.

As far as security on the campground was concerned, we probably had the safest spot. We backed on to the Graceland parking-lot which was patrolled by armed guards with dogs.

While America and I enjoyed an evening beer a man sang as he swept the parking-lot. 'Love me tender, love me true.... Hi, brother,' he said, spotting me.

'Hi, are you Elvis?'

'Why hell – no, I'm Moses...' He wolf-whistled. And went back to 'Love Me Tender'.

Next day I did our laundry. It was seven-thirty a.m. and the launderette was buzzing – full of women except for me. I grabbed the last free washer, stuffed some clothes into it and sat down with a magazine, trying to read but unable to stop listening to the conversation around me. From what I could glean, the women in the launderette were all from Charleston – and had a terrible, violent man in common. 'That darn Hugo, I'll never forget him – he really gave me a beating.'

'You know, I suffered more with Hugo than I did with any of the others,' said a second woman.

'He was so bad,' said a third. 'He took nearly everything I owned... I've never been whipped like that before.' Who was this Hugo? He sounded a monster.

I buried my head in my magazine and kept my ears tuned in. Soon, as the first one started up again, my curiosity was satisfied. 'Well, I've lived in South Carolina for thirty six years and I'm telling you, I have never experienced anything like that. Gracie was mean but Hurricane Hugo – man, he was the worst...' What a disappointment! I put down the magazine and left.

Having given the boys breakfast at six, I went alone to the bathroom for a shower while America supervised them in the playground. I shaved beneath the print of *Prince George's Favourite Things*, beside a youth who was rearranging his pony-tail into plaits. I watched enviously. I'd been going bald for years but, looking in the mirror, could now see the dome of my head. I had even less hair than I'd started with on this trip. Was it the sun? Or the nappy-stained panama? Or the nerve-shattering effect of the kids? Whatever the cause, after a shower, not only did my eyebrows take longer than my hair to dry – they even took longer to comb. But this wasn't only 'cause my barnet was getting thinner. It was because my eyebrows were getting thicker. They were like two triffids, stuck on my face – growing at a furious, unstoppable rate. I'd soon look like Leonid Brezhnev. *Poor Khelga!*

I took a deep breath, relaxed... and realised that (in spite of things) Memphis had actually been a lift. The pace of our trip was now more gentle and America, like Julia, was great with the kids. We'd certainly been lucky with most of our au pairs. Those who had stayed had not only been delightful (and a great help) but had also added a youthful, (additional) international, dimension to our household. But we had had some duffers. America first came to us after a French girl left.

Nicole from Normandy said, on arrival, that our house was small. Shortly afterwards, she accused Nicolai (then two) of being illogical. She spoke little English (but complained when I spoke French) and after two days lost her temper with Nicolai. We knew things wouldn't work out and, within a week, she'd left. But finding the right replacement took time. So while Khelga went to the office, I looked after the kids (and tried to work in the evening).

We registered with several agencies, received America's details, interviewed her in Saragossa on the phone and hired her. She was an instant success. (Having spent the previous summer working in Sizzling Sausages on Trafalgar Square – she spoke good English and knew London well. She also cooked a mean chipolata.) But only two months later her mother summoned her back to Spain to fly with the family to Managua. Her Nicaraguan grandmother had had a heart attack and they were going there immediately.

America announced she was leaving. Khelga was furious and with typical Russian frankness (Russians are accustomed to illness and tragedy) said: 'But she's not even dead yet. Can't you wait a while?'

America couldn't wait. She went to Nicaragua and to the family's embarrassment the grandmother recovered. Meanwhile, we hired Julia, who was also a success, but after returning to Spain, America wrote and said she was bored. When the motorhome trip came up I asked her if she would like to join us. Thankfully, she jumped at the opportunity.

Since our trip, the Louise Woodward case has been in the news.

My sympathies are with both sides but having employed several au pairs I would advise that if parents have any instinctive reservations, they should let the au pair go as soon as possible. The advantage of using an agency is that they usually work hard to find a replacement – especially if they haven't received their fee (the fact is, no matter how many glowing details they send, you don't know how someone will fit in, until they're living in your house). Apart from Nicole, we've had other bad experiences: an anorexic (who made it difficult to encourage the kids to eat); a girl who couldn't find Safeway after numerous accompanied trips there (not confidence-inspiring when you're leaving your kids with her); and a twenty-three-year-old who, the day after her arrival from Munich, said she preferred little girls — our lads' lack of interest in ribbons and frocks was going to make her life too challenging.

Friends have also had their share of problems: au pairs who need as much care as their own children; man-eaters; phone exploiters; drug-takers and a toilet-paper thief (she sneaked supplies out for friends in a flat). But whoever the person, parents must remember that for around forty pounds a week, plus board, au pairs are there to lend a hand. Not to be a substitute parent or cheap domestic. Relationships work when both sides get on well and are comfortable fulfilling each other's requirements. And although most au pairs come to Britain to improve their English, they must have fun too.

So as I prepared lunch while America amused the boys, I felt pleased she'd been able to join us.

23 Bill Clinton Country

We left Tennessee when we crossed the Mississippi. WELCOME TO ARKANSAS said a sign, HOME OF PRESIDENT BILL CLINTON.

Our first Arkansas campground was in Little Rock. In the reception area was a glass cabinet dedicated to the facts about Bill. From the cards on display I learnt that:

His favourite film is *High Noon* — but he's a fan of *Casablanca*.

He graduated from Hot Springs High School where he earned all-state honors on the saxophone.

He ranked fourth academically in his high-school class of 323 students.

He was elected governor of Arkansas at the age of 32.

He was born William Jefferson Blythe IV but took his surname from his late stepfather, Roger Clinton, who operated a Buick dealership in Hot Springs.

He was the forty-second governor of Arkansas and the forty-second United States President.

(I did not learn that he was the most libidinous US President since John F. Kennedy and was known as 'The Big Zipper').

The cabinet also displayed a personally signed letter from the White House. It thanked Larry (the campground owner) for 'all your support'. Around the cards were carefully arranged photos of Bill and Hillary. There were flattering facts about her too.

America made dinner. It was going to be Sausage Spanish Omelette but the Teflon on our saucepan was now so badly scratched that not even her 'Sizzling' training could stop it becoming Sausage Scrambled Egg.

The weather was hotter than it had been in Memphis. Humidity was also more intense. It took two hours to get the kids to sleep. The air-conditioning was not much help at night. If I kept it on, we froze. If I turned it off, we baked.

Next morning, we headed for a city park campground. I'd made a reservation in Burns Park, according to tourist leaflets the second largest city park in the United States (locals said the biggest was Encanto Park in Phoenix, Arizona — no one's disputed that yet).

At the campground entrance was a trailer. A cable ran across the entrance road setting off a bell each time a vehicle passed. When the bell rang a man called Bill came out. He was the husband of the campground manager, Lavada.

I registered and asked him if Burns Park water was drinkable (I'd read in a camping book that occasionally, in city parks, it's not). 'Put it this way,' said Bill. 'It's Little Rock city water and Bill Clinton did OK on it. If it's good enough for him, I think it's good enough for us...'

Burns Park is in North Little Rock, only about six miles from the downtown state capital but full of deer, racoons and squirrels and with the constant buzz and chatter of birds in the air. In front of the house were jars of coloured water. 'For the humming birds,' Lavada told us. 'It's sugar solution with food colouring. They can't leave it alone.'

The humming birds were enchanting. The size of a man's index finger, they looked more like tiny flying fish than birds. 'Ruby-throaters,' said Bill. 'But we get many different species here — red-headed peckerwoods, robins, jaybirds...'

'And of course chiggers,' sighed Lavada. 'Those nasty bugs you never see...'

During the kids' siesta, America and I cleaned the RV. Then she sat outside to read her paper. It was *El Nuevo Claridad* — the newspaper of the Spanish Communist party. 'Is that for your course?' I asked. (She was starting university the following October.)

'No. Personal interest...'

'Are you a communist?'

'Yes, I am.'

'Well, perhaps you could keep that quiet — especially as we go further west...'

Shopping in a local mall that evening (a nightmare to reach — we passed through endless suburban streets, full of frighteningly low branches), I bought some flypaper from Fred's Pharmacy. I explained the concept to the kids — they were fascinated.

'You see,' I said, pinning some to the ceiling. 'Flies land on this paper and get stuck. They can't get off the paper so they die. In the morning we'll find lots of dead mosquitoes and flies. Just you wait and see...'

Unfortunately it didn't work out like that. I got up for the loo in the middle of the night and walked right into the sticky paper. Before dawn I got up again and walked into the paper a second time. When the kids awoke there were no flies on the paper but my head was a sticky mess. (It took fifteen minutes to wash the glue off.)

One of the Burns Park children's play areas, about a mile from the campground, had some wonderful roundabouts and a huge slide in the form of a rocket. The boys spent the morning playing, then I cooked up lunch in the parking-lot (using the generator for the first time – with Cruise America you either pay an hourly rate or an upfront amount for unlimited use. I had opted for the former choice).

I served pork chops and microwaved vegetables but everything came out either dry or burnt. 'You're still a bad cook,' said Charlie. 'You *always* burn food...' (But it's not easy making lunch in a parking-lot.)

Next to the lot was a small waterpark. Charlie and I tried it but after a few minutes a thunderstorm began. Everyone was ordered out of the water so we left.

We adored Burns Park. We had plenty of space and it was so relaxing. One afternoon we ventured downtown. WELCOME TO LITTLE ROCK, said a sign, FIRST CAPITOL HOME OF PRESIDENT CLINTON.

Little Rock, political and financial centre of Arkansas, stands in the middle of the state. It first gained notoriety as a race-relations battleground in 1957 when, after the Supreme Court had ruled educational segregation unconstitutional, the state governor tried to prevent black students entering Central High School. Legal and physical battles followed and President Eisenhower had to send in troops to allow the first black students into school.

Its present notoriety stems from Bill's problems – Whitewater (a failed land development deal or 'big bunch o' legal garbage' as one Little Rock citizen described it to me) and alleged local sexual adventures Bill had before he moved to Washington. At the time we were there Monica Lewinsky was not a household name. Paula Jones was Clinton's legal headache. And she created a local bonanza. Little Rock hotel rooms were sold to TV networks to cover what was expected to be a juicy trial. When the court dismissed it the hotels kept the TV companies' one hundred-per-cent deposits. Rumour had it that one room at the Legacy (with a great view of the courthouse) had gone for fifteen thousand dollars.

But Paula Jones didn't lose out either. Kenneth Starr, the independent counsel investigating Whitewater had been looking for witnesses to provide a story of White House wrong-doing and obstruction. Frustrated, he authorised his prosecutors to enquire into every aspect of Clinton's past, including Paula Jones and other women. Monica Lewinsky denied a relationship but when Linda Tripp produced a tape in which she discussed an intimate affair she was catapulted into the investigation. What followed is history. Monica Lewinsky found global fame. Paula Jones received a huge out-of-court settlement from Clinton. And the Presidency survived.

City visitors can follow 'The Path To The Presidency – A Guided Tour Of Bill Clinton's Little Rock' which takes in everything from the governor's mansion, where he spent twelve years as governor; to the Rose law firm, where Hillary worked; to the gym in the YMCA of metropolitan Little Rock, where Bill worked out 'alongside his fellow Arkansans'.

We saw the governor's mansion (built between 1947 and 1950 and located in a 'historic district'), the state capitol (which looked familiar – it's a replica of the US Capitol in Washington DC) and the original 'little rock' (in Riverfront Park) after which the city was named. Then we got out of town.

Back at Burns Park we met a camping family. My accent provoked the usual interest, so I told them what I was doing and the father said he would like to try the same in Britain. 'So what's the motorhome scene like over there?' he asked.

'Don't know,' I said. 'But most motorhomes in Britain are half or even a third the size of yours because our roads are so much smaller.'

That seemed to dent his enthusiasm but later they passed us. Their RV stopped and the wife ran out. 'I just wanted to say,' she said, touching my arm, 'that I think what you're doing is beautiful. God bless you. Good luck. And have a wonderful trip...' She got back in the RV and they drove off.

The following afternoon we left too. We said goodbye to Bill and Lavada and headed for our next stop – Lake Ouachita State Park.

We arrived after dark and the office was closed. The park was poorly illuminated and we drove around several times, unable to find a free space. All camping areas were packed — with motorhomes, trailers, cars, motorbikes and boats. Finally, I found a space and tried to reverse in. But it was between two trees and my attempts in the darkness failed miserably. Luckily an old man came to our rescue.

'Need help?' he shouted.

'Certainly do...'

'One minute — I'll just get a flashlight.' He ran into his trailer, emerged with a torch, then guided me perfectly into the tight space.

'Thanks,' I said.

'You bet — want a beer?'

We had a beer at the campsite table. The helpful chap told me his name was Jack, that he was seventy-nine-and-a-half-years-old (and due to celebrate the 'Big Eight-Oh' in November) and from Baton Rouge in Louisiana. He was on a three-week motorhome vacation with his wife of fifty years, Dolly.

He had a kind face but was wearing an extremely vulgar T-shirt. BRAD'S BAR CASINO, it said. LIQUOR UP THE FRONT — POKER UP THE REAR. YOURS TO ENJOY. COME INSIDE.

'Like my T-shirt?' he asked, as I strained to read it.

'Very...er...amusing,' I said.

'Nah, you can be honest with me son, you know. It's not the kind of thing an English gentleman should like... Dolly's not mad on it either.'

92

24 TV Fame in Arkansas

I woke up next morning to find us in the middle of a forest by a lake. The morning sunlight was gently filtered through the trees. This was no Centerparc – this was for real. Lake Ouachita looked Edenic. Kids peddled bicycles, people paddled pedalos, fishermen fished (the lake teems with carp, pike and bream) and joggers ran through the trees. We trooped over to the Visitors' Center to find out about organised activities – a lecture on 'The Snakes of Arkansas'; 'Adventure Walks'; 'Painting for Kids'; 'Pedalo Races on the Lake'...

Campers were arriving and departing, many in three-unit combinations – a motorhome pulling a car which in turn towed a boat. Or a pick-up towing a trailer and a boat. Some of these units were driven by *very* old people. And the roads through the forest were difficult – narrow, twisting and overhung with branches. But no one seemed daunted. Nothing puts Americans off their vacation pleasures. I adored that spirit.

Most folk had a boat or a jet-ski. But we didn't have either so we spent the day swimming with what looked like the poorer campers – those without a craft (most of whom stayed in tents). As usual, my boys were soon scrounging toys.

In a playground we met Brandon Duane Conger, an eighteen-year-old from Shreveport, Louisiana who told us, nostalgically, that his family vacationed at Lake Ouachita every summer and that he had played in this very playground since he was four.

'It's certainly a whole lot nicer than Shreveport,' he informed us. 'I live in an area which is full of hoodlums. You hear shootings all night... Here you can take it easy and relax by the water – away from the chaos and the gangs.'

He said he was getting out of Shreveport. 'I'm joinin' the army – as a computer operator. They send me to school and spend forty thousand dollars to train me up. Then they give me a bunch o' cash and I become a private first-class – that's the lowest ranking soldier allowed to give orders. But it's a start. Every member of my family has gone into the army for the last five generations. Heh – you religious? I'm in the Church of the Nazarene...'

We wished Brandon well and left him in the playground. Back at our site some neighbours had moved in next door – Maggy and Bobby, the Bowdens from Cleveland, Ohio. I knew they were the Bowdens from Cleveland, Ohio because a portable wooden sign that

they'd placed in front of their RV told me so. I wasn't sure I liked this self-proclaimed matiness. One thing I knew – it certainly wasn't British. I couldn't imagine myself ever putting a sign in front of our RV which said 'Matt, Charles and Nicolai, the Collinses from London, England'. I waved at Maggy and Bobby, smiling as I entered the RV. I didn't want to talk. I wanted to hear a British adult voice. Anything: Chris Evans; even the shipping forecast.

I dug out my short-wave radio and unwound the wire aerial. Then I stretched it across the ceiling, pushed it through a window, went outside and attached it to the branch of a tree. Back in the RV I tuned into the World Service. Reception was perfect. John Peel's scouse drawl was peppering the space between his usual, youthful obscure numbers. But requests were coming in from Delhi, Johannesburg, Cairo and Hong Kong rather than London, Manchester, Leeds or Glasgow... Soon, a more traditional BBC voice announced that Gianni Versace had been murdered in in Florida – *by a serial killer still on the loose.* I switched off the radio and prayed that the killer stayed in Florida.

Stupidly, I didn't disconnect the aerial, so when I tried to leave next morning, the radio was pulled through the window before crashing on to the ground outside. It wasn't damaged but batteries were everywhere and I had to suffer mutterings from my tiny children who seemed incredulous that anyone could be quite so stupid. We set off after a final, wistful gaze at the lake. Two eagles were circling it gracefully.

On Route 227 I pulled in at a small, ancient-looking gas station. A pick-up stopped and a gangly man in a filthy white baseball hat, smoking a cigarette with a dangling, red-hot head of ash got out. He placed a can on the ground and proceeded to fill it with gas. But he concentrated so little on what he was doing (focusing on his pick-up passenger and gesticulating wildly as he spoke) that most of the gas slopped on to the forecourt. As he filled up he sucked on his cigarette, making the red-hot ash-head dangle more. I'd wanted a tankful but hastily settled for four dollars' worth instead. I ran into the station shop, slapped some bills on to the counter and asked the cashier if she found him dangerous.

'Sure,' she drawled. 'We're all gonna go up in smoke someday...'
'But don't you have a 'No Smoking' sign?'
'No, sir, we don't.'

'Why not?' I asked.

'Cos we're all a bunch of rednecks round here...'

I got back in the RV and sped away.

You hear a lot about rednecks in the South. The term was first applied to non-skilled Southern labourers (who got red necks working outside). These days it's widely used but modern definitions had so far eluded me. Then I bought a tape by Georgian comedian, Geoff Foxworthy. It was titled *The Redneck Test*.

According to Geoff:

> If your richest relative has just bought a new home and you've helped him take the wheels off it... you might be a redneck.
>
> If your idea of quality entertainment is a video and a six pack... you might be a redneck.
>
> If your family tree don't fork – you're *definitely* a red neck.

Geoff made me chuckle as I drove across the States. If you've seen the South, I can recommend his style.

A couple of hours after almost being blown up at the gas station we pulled into a shopping mall and witnessed some police drama. Two guys were being arrested by three cops from three separate cars. They were made to stand against a wall, spread their legs and put their hands in the air while the cops thrashed around with their guns. Then the men were handcuffed and taken away in a swirl of lights and sirens.

'Wow,' I said to someone who'd been watching the incident. 'What did they do? Attempt a shoot out?'

'Nah,' said the man. 'Just get drunk...'

Elsewhere in the parking-lot a crowd of people stood by a truck. A sign was displayed by a table. THE THV NEIGHBOURHOOD WEATHER TOUR WILL BE HERE AT THE ALBERT PIKE HOT SPRINGS HARVEST FOODS ON FRIDAY JULY 18. MEET METEOROLOGIST ED BUCKNER, EAT SOME GREAT FOOD, TALK WITH 11 LISTENS (the TV channel's comment line) AND ENTER TO WIN GREAT PRIZES.

I ran back to the motorhome. 'Free grub,' I said. 'Come on, let's go...' America stayed in the RV.

While we joined the food queue I picked a card up from the table. TODAY'S THV, it said, under a smiling face, ED BUCKNER. On the back was a resumé: 'Ed joined Today's THV in 1996 anchoring the

Trooper Moore reassures Charlie that Dad's not going to be arrested

Roadside refreshment in Texas

Halt! View through the RV windscreen of Julia directing me

Trusty assistants see to the hook-ups

Charlie chats with Bert, our
Chatanooga Choo Choo
Engine driver

Sliding around the Texas Steak Ranch on Booster Seats

Bill explains the roof repair to Charlie

The boys spray a Cadillac

Distracted Dad in Vegas

Tussling under Lincoln
in Washington DC

Charlie hides his terror from a Grand Canyon Railway Cowboy

America, the boys and the Grand Canyon Railway Locomotive

Posing at Four Corners

Cruising through Colorado at twilight

Making 'Son-of-a-gun' stew at the Oklahoma Hall of Fame

Meeting Smokey.
What's Nicolai's
wet patch?

weekday five, six and ten p.m. newscasts. He is a broadcast meteorologist and a member of the National Weather Association. Ed won an Associated Press award for best spot news coverage of the south-east Texas flood of 1994...'

I queued for food and soon had hot dogs, ice-creams and drinks for three. Nicolai lunged at my booty. 'For goodness' sake, wait,' I said. 'Please be patient for one minute.'

'So what's an English guy doing here in Arkansas?' I turned round. It was Buckner himself.

'Well, Ed,' I replied, creepily. 'Your fame has spread so far that we've heard about you in England. So I just had to come and say hello...'

'Gee!' he exclaimed. 'You wanna be interviewed? You wanna go live over Arkansas?... Guys, this is our next interviewee... You ever been on American TV, sir?'

'No, Ed, I haven't but I'd love to...' Ed's crew positioned us and a young researcher said we'd be interviewed during his next link. 'OK, just be real natural when Ed talks to you,' she advised. But the kids were restless and demanding more food.

'You want another bratwurst, boys?' asked Ed. 'More food, guys, please.' Three hot dogs immediately arrived.

Nicolai and Charlie grabbed theirs but just as I was about to receive mine the chef had a sudden TV brainwave: 'Heh, Ed,' he suggested, eagerly. 'Why don't we hand it over when we're live?'

'Neat idea,' said Ed, smoothing his hair. 'OK, we're on. Everyone ready?... Going live in ten... stand by...'

The camera ran and Ed did his piece. 'Well,' he said beaming. 'Here we are at Harvest Foods in Hot Springs and we've got someone with us from out o' state. What's your name, sir, and where are you from?'

'My name's Matthew Collins and I'm from London, England.'

'And what are you doing in Arkansas?'

'I'm crossing America in a motorhome with my two children and we're almost half way through our trip...' A bratwurst was thrust into my hand. 'Thanks,' I said. 'We think Arkansas is beautiful...'

He turned to the boys, asked them their names and how they liked America (he didn't get much response as their mouths were stuffed with food). Then he said: 'Well, thanks to Matthew, Charles and Nicolai from London, England. And good luck with your trip, guys. Now, here's the weather for the Hot Springs area: It's gonna be hot, hot, hot, with temperatures up in the nineties. But that hurricane's still moving across from Louisiana...'

The researcher took us aside and thanked us quietly as Ed finished forecasting. Then he came over and thanked us himself. As we were talking a man approached. 'Excuse me, Ed – I'm a preacher at the local baptist church. If you'd ever like to come along, we'd all be mighty pleased to see you.' And he handed over his business card to Ed.

'Why thank you, sir,' the weatherman replied courteously. 'I appreciate that – I really do.'

'So what about this hurricane in Louisiana?' I asked, when the preacher had moved on. 'Is it going to affect us?'

'Which way you travelling?'

'Directly west...'

'Well, you should be OK – it's going south-east... But tell me about England? You don't get many hurricanes, I suppose. Just fog and rain, huh? Gee, I gotta get there sometime – you got so much history and stuff... But also, you gotta tell me... What about your English weathermen...?

I told him my wife thought most of the BBC guys looked like pensioners, and mentioned that Michael Fish had famously failed to predict the 1987 British hurricane. Ed was amazed. 'Is that so?' he asked. 'Does he still have a job?'

I said that, as a civil servant, Michael Fish probably had a job for life, but conventional BBC meteorologists had nevertheless been under pressure from glamorous competition on commercial channels. One blonde, I said, had even made a career on the entertainment side of TV. She was always on game shows and had a famously turbulent love life. 'Now, that *is* interesting...' Ed replied, pondering. Then, he took my hand and said briskly, 'Well, it's been great talking to you, Matt. Good luck with your trip.' And he disappeared into a van – away from preachers, autograph seekers and us.

Before returning to our RV the chef asked if we wanted yet more food. It was free, we were still hungry, we *had* done an interview. 'Great,' I said, appreciatively, 'thanks.'

'Well, I'll be one second with your hot dogs but while you're waiting, would you care to fill out one of these?' He pointed to some papers on the table.

They were market research forms. *Which station do you turn to for your daily news?* asked the first question. I put Today's THV. *If you answered Today's THV*, asked the second, *How do you rate the newscasts?* I put excellent. *In severe weather who do you turn to for weather information?* I put Today's THV. *Who are your favourite Arkansas television personalities?* I put Ed Buckner. *What is your opinion of these personalities?* Next to Ed Buckner, I put EXCELLENT (adding: DEFINITELY SHOULD HAVE HIS OWN SHOW).

I signed off: 'Matt, a Brit — somewhere in America', and put the form in a box for 'a chance to win great prizes from Harvest Foods'.

Beside me a man was holding his questionnaire; as my eyes scanned it I noticed his answers. When asked for his opinion of local TV people, he'd scrawled only AVERAGE for Ed Buckner. Worse, he'd added traitorously that his favourite TV weather personality was some bloke called 'Barry Brandt'.

'OK...' said the chef. 'There you go, guys — enjoy.' He loaded me up with more hot dogs, drinks and ice-creams and wished us all a wonderful trip.

25 Brief (Supermarket) Encounter

We walked back to the RV gorging ourselves. I needed some groceries so I left the boys with America, ran around the supermarket and queued to pay. Then I remembered I didn't have olive oil so I went back looking for 'Condiments' but couldn't find it. A petite, glamorous, forty-something woman, with a lithe figure in T-shirt, jeans and cowboys boots, sauntered into view. I smiled at her and scanned the shelves again. 'Excuse me, please,' I said, ridiculously polite, in a completely over-the-top English voice (I sounded like Trevor Howard in *Brief Encounter*). 'You don't by any chance happen to know where olive oil is, do you?'

She returned the smile. 'I'm sorry,' she said. 'I'm after mayonnaise myself.'

I handed her some Hellman's and she turned to a Harvest Foods assistant. 'Sir, could you find this gentleman some olive oil...' While the assistant searched, we made our way to separate cash desks and she asked me across my shopping where I was from.

'England,' I said.

'Thought so,' she replied. 'You're not from Birming–*Ham*, are you?'

'Um, no I'm not.' (So much for my Trevor Howard accent.)

'It's just that I've got a friend from Birming–*Ham* and you sound just like him...'

'Great,' I thought. (Well done, Trevor...) 'Where are *you* from?'

'Las Vegas,' she said proudly. 'Ever been there?'

'No, but I want to see it.'

'You must,' she said. 'There is *so much* to do...' The Harvest Foods man brought my olive oil.

'Thanks... Did you stay long in Vegas?'

'Born and raised ...'

'Wow,' I said impressed. 'That must have been fun.'

'Sure was – I was a child entertainer. I used to dance with Dean Martin, Frank Sinatra, Sammy Davies, all those guys... They were great, great times...'

'Wow,' I said again. 'And do you still dance?'

'Not professionally. Now I teach.'

We paid for our shopping and left Harvest Foods. After lifting her bags out of her trolley, she booted it away with an athletic kick. 'So what's an English guy doin' all alone in Hot Springs?'

Momentarily tempted to deny the existence of my children, I said: 'I'm crossing America... driving coast to coast...'

'Neat!' she said, smiling.

'Yeh... in a motorhome...'

'Great!'

'Yeh, it is... Just me and the boys...'

'Just you and the boys? And are *you and the boys* stayin' in Hot Springs?'

'Well... I'm not actually certain. I'll have to ask the boys... '

'Uh huh...'

'Yeh...'

'Good...'

'Well, actually the boys are my children. They're three and four years old. They're just over there...'

'And that your wife?' she asked, spotting America inside with them.

'No, she's my au pair girl. She helps with the children... My wife is back home in England...'

'Back home in England? What's she doin' there?'

'Working...'

'And paying for your trip? You've got things pretty well worked out.'

'Well, it's not quite like that...'

'No..?' She raised her eyebrows, threw her bags into her Jeep and slammed the door. 'Well, you have a great trip, sir. And say hello to Vegas for me.'

'I will.' We shook hands then she got in the car. I returned to my brood and she screeched away.

26 Heat Problems in Hot Springs

At The Gorge campground in Hot Springs National Park I needed several attempts to reverse into my space – it was narrow and overhung with branches.

By the time we were parked I was sweating profusely. America did the hook-ups and I lifted the kids up out of their seats. The motorhome next to us had its engine running and exhaust fumes soon filled our RV. I looked inside the other vehicle. A middle-aged couple were sitting at a table reading magazines. I waited for them to turn the engine off. They didn't. So I knocked on their door.

'Excuse me,' I said. 'Would you mind turning your engine off. It's just that we're next door and your exhaust is coming through our windows.'

'Oh...' said the man, puzzled. 'We were just so–o–oh hot...' The couple had two large, roof-mounted air-conditioning units as well as the engine's air-conditioning running.

'So, where y'all from?' asked the woman brightly.

'England,' I replied.

'Wonderful,' she said. 'I've always wanted to go there. We're from Tampa in Florida.'

'Great,' I said. Her husband killed the engine. 'OK, thanks for turning it off.'

Two minutes later there was a knock at the door. It was our neighbours. 'Hi,' said the wife. 'I'm sorry about that bother with the engine. My name's Veronica and I'd like you to have this delicious blackcurrant jelly made right here in Arkansas...'

'If we were feeling really Christian we'd give you some of our wonderful Arkansas honey, too,' added the husband. 'But we've only got one jar of that, so... My name is Dale, by the way...'

'Matthew,' I replied.

'May I say how cute your little boy is,' stated Veronica. 'My, he looks so British – he's just a typical, little British boy.'

'Actually, he's half Russian. His mother's from Moscow...'

'Well, to be honest, he's got a kinda Russian look, too. And look, there's your other one... Now he's a real Russian-lookin' little fella...' Then she gushed: 'You know, we got a good friend in Russia. He went out there, met a Russian girl and fell in love. It was beautiful but then he got married and took *her* nationality. I dunno what he's gonna do if they ever shut the doors on that place – he's never gonna get out...'

Dale told us that this was their first vacation for ten years. They'd spent the previous decade doing up a house. 'You know it was so hard coming back from work and then doing jobs every night. In the end it got to us and we were ill...'

'We've got chronic fatigue syndrome,' said Veronica, almost proudly. 'I don't think you get that in England. You're real lucky 'cos it's terrible...'

'Is that ME?' I asked.

'Don't know,' said Dale. 'Maybe that's what you call it over there...'

They then told us that their RV was rented – just like ours – and invited us in for a peek. Two small dogs were sitting on the sofa. 'Shetland collies,' said Veronica. 'This one's Laddy and this is Mandy...'

'How do they travel?' asked Charlie. 'Do they have seat belts?'

'No, honey, they have a crate.'

'You mean a cage,' said Charlie, pointing to the object under the table.

'You could say that, honey, but we call it a crate... Well, we'd offer y'all something to drink but we've only got these two Cokes... Would you like a cookie or something?'

'No, it's OK, thank you, Veronica. I'm not really hungry.' After our free food the kids weren't hungry either. We returned to our own RV and all went to bed.

Next morning, after Dale and Veronica had left, new neighbours pulled in next to us – a young mum and dad and a toddler called Ryan. They had a pick-up and trailer but, shortly afterwards, the dad rolled up on a shiny 900cc Kawasaki motorcycle. He was soon riding it around the campground, the toddler sitting in front of him, neither bothering with helmets. 'Why don't *you* get a motorbike?' said Charlie.

'Want a go?' asked the father. And to Charlie's delight he gave him a ride. Nicolai meanwhile played on Ryan's quad-bike – a child's four-wheeler with electric motor. The family was from San Antonio, Texas. Tom, the dad, worked in the gas exploration industry and had just finished a contract. He'd bought the toys that morning – one each for himself and the kid – before he went to work in Alaska.

Soon we were discussing Clinton. 'I don't care about the guy screwin' around,' said Tom (who revealed he had two children from two previous relationships). 'But you know what I don't like about government in this country? They take our tax dollars and give them to those on welfare... You know how much tax I pay? Twenty-seven per cent! That means every week, I work almost a day and a half for free... Why should I do that?'

Tom seemed convinced that America was the highest taxing country in the world and that US welfare benefits were obscenely generous. 'You know what I think should happen to all those on welfare – they should goddamn fry...' After exchanging final pleasantries, we left the family to their toys.

Hot Springs is a spa town within the National Park whose thermal waters have attracted visitors since Native Americans used the area as a territory-dispute-solving zone. Early settlers created a primitive resort but after the arrival of the railroads it became a European-style spa. During the 1920s and 1930s the mayor reputedly ran a gambling syndicate worth thirty million dollars a year. Punters included Al Capone and Bugsy Malone.

Its popularity waned in the 1950s. But interest in the place revived after Clinton's first election in 1992 (he lived there between 1953 and 1964). We drove past his flag-festooned, former home, a few houses up from Stubby's Barbecue.

If only the kids had not been so bad-tempered (humidity was intense) I'd have stopped at one of the bathhouses. 'It's boring here,' said Charlie. 'You're not going to have a massage. We want to go and see some cowboys!' So I settled for a bottle of fresh spring water, filled up from a National Park fountain. Then we hit the road for cowboy country.

27 Into the Wild West

Historically, Arkansas belongs to the South (it sided with the Confederacy during the Civil War) but geographically it's the start of the Great Plains – the flat expanse of middle America. Back in the late nineteenth century this was pioneer country – the original Wild West, home to trappers, traders, hunters and explorers.

'As you go west, folks become crazy,' an old man had told me in Virginia. 'Most descend from those who didn't make it back east...' Travelling through the Ouachita National Forest I saw his point.

A car full of men overtook me at speed. They were mouthing insults and making obscene gestures. As they continued ranting into the distance, the driver hit a curve too fast. The car screeched to the other side of the road, then stopped menacingly and reversed. As it approached me the occupants looked frenzied with fury.

I slammed into reverse myself and using every mirror (and America to navigate me through the rear windscreen) drove backwards madly until I reached a small (but, thankfully, busy) gas station. The car ahead stopped then drove on again, the occupants still mouthing obscenities. What had I done? US7 is narrow in parts and people loathe being stuck behind RVs. But they had overtaken easily. Perhaps it was my Washington State number plates. Or maybe they were out of their heads on drugs.

I bought some gas and entered the station's own tiny general store. It was full of seats. 'So people can talk,' said the owner. 'Makes it kind o' friendly. Only problem is we get folks who spend a dollar and then hang around for three hours...'

I told her about the men in the car. 'Yeh, that don't surprise me. We get some nuts around here.' Then I pressed ahead, stopping briefly in London.

London, Arkansas, that is – population: 825. I had to get a photo of us in front of the town's welcome sign. As America took it, a woman approached, excitedly. 'Y'all from England? I guessed you were. We took similar pictures when we visited London, England – to show the the folks back in London, Arkansas...'

Further up US7 the landscape became more barren, resembling the West we'd seen in movies. Roadside notices advertised 'Cows and Bulls For Sale'. We even saw a 'Cowboy Café'.

At Fort Smith, on the Oklahoman border, a sign at the local Arbys restaurant told us it was a hundred and five degrees outside. Until 1875, when Charles Isaac Parker – the 'Hanging Judge' – arrived, this was a riotous pioneer town, a refuge for bandits and robbers. Parker had two hundred marshals round up the fugitives and in twenty-one years sentenced a hundred and sixty to death, personally witnessing seventy-nine hangings. The Historic Center on Rogers Avenue features remains of the original fort, Parker's courtroom, the jail and some gallows. I explained the story to the boys who were fascinated. 'Can *we* see some hangings?' asked Nicolai.

Old Main Street was our first sight of a genuine cowboy town. Part of it is a stretch of restored buildings, featured in numerous westerns. After photos we went to a supermarket. Turning round suddenly, the checkout cashier accidentally hit Charlie. 'Gee, I am *so* sorry Pumpkin – I'm really sorry about that. Are you OK, pumpkin? You poor little thing...'

Charlie smirked, hardly noticing his knock. '*Pumpkin?*' he exclaimed. 'I'm not a *pumpkin*, am I, daddy?'

'Well,' said the cashier, amiably. 'That's what I've always called *my* little boy. Still do, and he's forty-four now...'

As I checked in for the night at the KOA in Sallisaw, Oklahoma, Nicolai toyed with items in the store (Charlie stood beside me, sagely, at the desk). 'Quit playing with those toys, son,' said the manager, sternly. Then turning to me he added: 'These kids, you know – no one to control them.'

'He's my son,' I said.

'Oh, he your son, too? I didn't realise. That's OK, then. If he breaks anything, you'll just have to pay for it.'

On the check-in desk was a collection box for pennies. 'If you have one, leave one. If you need one, take one,' said a label.

Beside the collection box a list of aphorisms was displayed on the desk. 'God is like VO5 hairspray,' said one. 'He holds through all kinds of weather.' 'God is like Frosties,' said another. 'He's Grrreeeaaat...'

Settling Nicolai down that night, I massaged his forehead to relax him. 'You like having your forehead massaged, don't you, Nicolai?'

'Yes,' he replied. 'And I like Pepsi, too...'

28 Oklahoma, Men of Leisure and Cowboys

The boys were looking forward to 'Local-Homa'. This was the start of real cowboy country. But guide books were not promising about the state capital. 'During the 1930s,' said one (written before the downtown bombing), 'Oklahoma City was sprayed with oil... Today a working well remains on the capitol building's grounds. But that's about all activity downtown...'

Oklahomans are often the butt of jokes – outsiders refer to them as 'Okies'. But car registration plates state 'Oklahoman and Proud' and a leaflet I collected at the city KOA attempted to counter any negative images.

> The ingenuity and innovation of Oklahoma City residents is apparent in the birth of the aviation and oil industries and lives on in the shopping cart and parking meter...

> Sylvan Goldman invented the shopping cart in 1955, after standing in his Humpty Dumpty store watching women struggle with their groceries. Today, a bronze statue in the Omniplex Museum honours the founder of a strong Oklahoman manufacturing business...

> There was more: 'In 1935 former newspaperman, Carl Magee, invented the first parking meter, providing a solution to parking problems for Oklahoma City and the entire nation.' (We British had twenty-three more meter-free years – they arrived in London in 1958.)

That evening, while I tidied up like a proud little househusband, role reversal seemed to be endemic when a woman in her sixties slipped on white overalls and slid under the RV opposite ours while a man waited attentively beside it. 'Get me a wrench Johnny,' she ordered. Johnny trotted off, found her the wrench, crouched down and passed it over. After a few minutes she crawled out. 'OK, those stabilisers should be fine now.' She removed her overalls and re-entered the RV.

Johnny and I were soon chatting. It turned out he wasn't the woman's husband. 'Yeh, she's a great mechanic... She's a farmer's wife but he doesn't like these RV trips. Says they make him constipated. Well, you can't please everyone – but she really loves 'em. So she comes while he stays at home. She drives too. And she's as good at drivin' as she is at fixin' things.'

The mechanic was one of five women travelling with Johnny. He took me on board and presented me to his team. They were all in their mid-sixties. Johnny was at least a decade older. He had things worked out. Was this the future for my generation?

At the dinette table two women chopped vegetables while another (the mechanic) studied maps. 'Well,' he said, taking me through to the kitchen, 'this is my wife, Betsy. She does the cookin'... And this is Trish. She's Betsy's sister and does the dishes. Lauren and Suzie, there, have been friends of ours for years. They keep things clean and do odd jobs. The one with the maps, as you know, is our mechanic. Her name is Freda and she's also our driver. I used to drive but since she's been with us I don't even do that.'

'So what do you now?' I asked.

'Just take things easy and find people to talk to. Well, they wouldn't want me in their way.'

Johnny and I got out of the way by taking the children to the playground. He informed me that he was a seventy-seven-year-old retired Mississippi lumberman who had served in Britain during World War II. 'I remember London,' he said nostalgically, 'Although I haven't been back since. Man, there was so much smog – you could hardly see your hand in front of you...'

I asked him what England was like for a GI during the war. 'Did you date British girls? Did you have lots of nylons?'

'Oh boy, you had to have your nylons. If you didn't have your nylons, you wouldn't get the girls...'

Later I asked if he had fought.

'You know, I was going to do one of the landings but I tore a thigh muscle. So I never left England. But boy, I adored London in 1945. I'd love to go back. Do they still sell fish and chips in newspaper?'

As one of his women called him to supper I went to feed my own boys. I served a hastily made concoction – tuna and sweetcorn with mayonnaise in pitta bread. Nicolai behaved badly. He spilt his water, wouldn't eat his food and, as a party piece, stuck an index finger up his nose. 'Take it out!' I bellowed. I removed the finger but then he started having trouble breathing.

'Oh no!' said America. 'He's got sweetcorn stuck up his nostril!'
We stood him on the table and tried unsuccessfully to fish it out.

Then America fetched her tweezers and extracted it. 'Stupid boy!' I said, furious but relieved. 'Never put food (or anything) up your nose.'

Once the kids were tucked up, America phoned home. It was early morning in Spain. When she returned her face was joyful. The singer of her favourite Spanish rock band, Doctor Explosion (great Spanish name), to whom she'd been writing on the Internet for months had finally replied to her e-mails. And one of her friends had spotted the drummer of the very same band, in her favourite Saragossa bar. Stunned by this news I went to bed.

'When are we going to the dockyards?' asked Nicolai at six a.m. He meant the stockyards — where Oklahoman cowboys gather for livestock sales. I'd promised we'd see some stomping cattle.

It wasn't long before I was cruising around the city, quite lost. Pulling over to study my map, I noticed a fence ahead festooned with Americana. I drove further up. It was covered in baseball hats, car registration plates, T-shirts, whistles, photographs, flags and flowers... This was the site of the former Alfred P. Murrah building. The decorations were tributes to the hundred and sixty-eight victims of the Oklahoma City bombing.

Only a few weeks before on Hilton Head Island I'd read the lead story in the local newspaper: 'Timothy McVeigh Gets Death'.

I got out of the vehicle to read some tributes. The kids wanted to come but before I could even undo their seatbelts a cop had stuck his head through the front passenger window. 'You can't stop by a federal building, sir — pull-up in that lot around the corner...'

I re-parked and we walked to the fence. It surrounded a large grassy area. The remains of the bombed building had been demolished. All that was left was part of the parking-lot.

'Why are there so many toys here?' asked Charlie.

'They're presents to children... who died when a bomb went off here...'

'Who did it?' he asked.

'A horrible man...'

'What was his name?'

'Timothy McVeigh...'

'But Timothy's a nice name...'

'Yes... But he was a horrible man...'

'Did he *look* horrible, daddy?'

'No, he didn't, Charlie...'

'Well if he didn't look horrible, *why* was he horrible?'

'Well, that's the problem. Some horrible people look like normal people. That's why you have to be careful with people you don't know...'

Charlie reflected while I examined the tributes. 'Christy Jenkins. You always had to be first — first to be married, first to have children, first to say goodbye. 24 March 1963 — 19 April 1995.'

Flags, T-shirts and photographs were inscribed. 'In honor and loving memory of Steven Curry,' said one message. 'You have been in the presence of God for two years but your memory is with us every day. Monday 2 June 1997 — Guilty Verdict Read in Denver.'

The fence was covered with tributes from all over America. Two years after the event, people were still arriving to pay their respects. The effect of the bombing on the American collective psyche must have been absolutely massive. (But little did I realise, here in Oklahoma, that we were only weeks away from a different kind of tragedy, a royal one which was to affect the collective *British* psyche and bring millions flocking, with tributes, to London.)

We returned to the parking-lot. The kids could no longer resist the temptation to pull toys from the fence and I could take no more grief. *En route* to the RV, we passed a message daubed on a building: GOD CAN FORGIVE TIM IF TIM TURNS. We picked up the Interstate and drove to the stockyards. We parked next to a cattle truck, walked over metal bridges which crossed the endless cattle pens and entered a small amphitheatre.

In the seats were several dozen cowboys, all wearing stetsons, chewing, chatting, dozing and talking on phones. One at a time cows or bulls entered the arena. They'd emerge from a trap door, a Mexican cow-hand (standing, protected, behind a screen) would swish them on the rump with an over-sized fly swat and then they would snort, stomp and turn before exiting through another trap door. We took a front seat. Charlie was nervous, Nicolai entranced. Giant, snorting bulls stomped their hooves only inches from us.

After half an hour I was ready to leave but Nicolai wanted to stay. He was captivated — by the men in big hats, the auctioneer's banter, the bang of the hammer, and of course the stomping, snorting cattle. We had ten more minutes then left.

As we walked over a bridge a cowboy from the auction room strode up to us. 'Don't let your sons grow up to be cowboys,' he warned (there wasn't much chance of that in West Kensington). 'Keep them wearing tennis shoes and reading books...' He'd been selling stock. 'A cowboy's life is not an easy one...'

'Are prices *that* bad?' I asked.

'Let's say you could do better... They've fallen consistently for a year. To be really honest though, they're not *so* bad right now. Feed costs have been constant and stores are paying good bucks for most good stock. So things aren't as bad as they were....'

He'd been selling bulls. 'Those that have gone infertile or lost the urge. They'll go for baloney or sausage meat. Yep, that's what happens to them old bulls. They make that processed meat you buy.'

Before he strode on, I asked him to recommend a local steakhouse (preferably one which didn't serve processed meat). His reply was instant: 'Well, you can't do better than the Cattlemen's Café – it's by the gates of the stockyards.' I thanked him for the tip and said goodbye. 'You bet. And keep your sons reading those books...'

The Cattlemen's Café, which has served steaks since 1910 (and was lost and won in a game of crap in 1945) was heaving with cowboys – and office workers, doctors, lawyers, business people, shopkeepers, estate agents, college lecturers and tourists. The menu said a Republican 'darn near once got in' but then contradicted itself when it stated that George Bush, when president, had ordered the Cattlemen's T-bone – 'two steaks in one...the full-flavoured sirloin and impeccably tender filet' (maybe he'd been posing as a Democrat).

We settled for the modest five-ounce lunch steaks (Nicolai and Charlie shared one), the smallest and cheapest available. But they were good. No, they were *great*. The plates heaved with accompaniments and our meal for four was under thirty dollars.

After lunch we drove to the Cowboy Hall of Fame. This is a gallery dedicated to the art and heritage of the old West. But it also has a kids' section and fascinating artefacts. One was a nineteenth-century chuck wagon, complete with shelves, drawers and cookware. 'Look,' said America. 'The first RV.'

We read the ingredients for 'son-of-a-gun' stew: 'Half a pound of beef; quarter of a pound of beef fat; one and a half pounds of marrow gut; three to four pounds of heart; one to two pounds of liver; one set of brains; three to four pounds of sweetbreads; one pancreas....' 'A cowboy's diet lacked certain important vitamins,' said the caption, 'but was never short of meat.'

113

There was, naturally, a section dedicated to John Wayne. A TV showed a loop of movie clips. 'Kill! Kill!' said Nicolai as Wayne shot his foes.

In the children's section was a stuffed cow – a Texan long-horned steer. At first the kids patted it. Then they got silly. 'Look, daddy,' said Charlie. 'I've got my hand up his bottom.'

'Look, daddy,' said Nicolai. 'I've got my hand on his zuzu...'

'Well, kids will be curious,' said a smiling attendant. 'That's why it's here ... I mean that's how they learn. Heh, you guys wanna dress up as cowboys?' Her name was Betty Davis and, like the ladies in the Memphis Pyramid, she and her colleague (also called Betty) were retired locals, working voluntarily.

Betty Davis led the kids to a stash of cowboy clothes. Soon they were wearing stetsons, waistcoats and over-sized boots with spurs. While they had a shoot-out, I talked to the Bettys.

'Guess who we've got coming to Oklahoma in the Fall?' challenged Betty Davis.

'I don't know...'

'Fer–gie...' she said, proudly.

'Lucky you,' I muttered, ungraciously.

'It's gonna be huge. Tickets for the dinner are thousands of dollars each... How *is* your royal family at the moment?'

'Well, let's say that Fergie's not the most popular member,' I replied authoritatively. 'The British are not exactly proud of her...'

'Well,' said Betty Two, 'we all have our shame. I mean look at our president. What a disgrace!... Of course, Betty and I are both Republicans...'

'Yes, it's strange how so much dirt flies his way,' I added provocatively. 'And none of it seems to stick.'

'It's disgusting,' said Betty D. 'I mean, Clinton's done everything. Look at poor old Nixon – he had to resign over *one* single thing...'

'Hmmm...' I said, approaching the kids. They loved this section. We sat in front of an animatronic cowboy and listened to Wild West songs. Then it was time to move on. We said goodbye to the Bettys and I bought each boy a revolver-shaped comb. It was 'Kill! Kill! Kill!' as we drove further west.

114

29 Texan Steaks and Cadillacs

After an hour I saw a grey-haired, pony-tailed figure, standing dejectedly on the Interstate, trying to thumb a lift in the haze. It was burning out there – up in the nineties. 'Poor guy,' I thought, sitting in air-conditioned comfort. 'Maybe I should stop and pick him up.' I carried on driving, feeling vaguely guilty, until a sign appeared: WARNING – HITCH-HIKERS MAY BE ESCAPING INMATES.

As we progressed west temperatures kept creeping higher still. Even with the air-conditioning on maximum, the kids were having an increasing problem sleeping. That night, at El Reno KOA, I lay with Nicolai for an hour, massaging his head, trying to relax him into slumber. Charlie's needs were different. I had to *bore* him to sleep.

Khelga, Julia and America all specialised in conventional children's stories. But they're not my bag at all. So, just as my dad and I had done when I was small, Charlie and I discussed things (until he nodded off). Like what I'd done on my travels – eaten bear in Alaska; hang-glided from a mountain; had a gun put to my head in Italy. Then, after exhausting my own repertoire, I would plunder my dad's.

'When grandpa was a boy, a very long time ago, he was extremely silly and tried to shoot a mouse with an airgun... But he missed and shot the dog's bowl...' Charlie loved that one. I couldn't match it. Nor could I top several others. 'One day, grandpa was naughty at school. People were very strict in the olden days so his teacher hit him with a stick. Grandpa went home crying and told his daddy. But when he heard that grandpa had been naughty at school, his daddy hit him as well.' He adored that too but his favourites were about Egypt during the war: 'When grandpa was in Egypt during the war, he was *incredibly* silly. Do you know what he did? He went fishing for crocodiles in the River Nile and nearly got his bottom bitten off...' We discussed the details of every single story until Charlie finally fell asleep.

But sometimes, when I thought he was sleeping, he would suddenly sit up like Frankenstein. 'Daddy, tell me about when grandpa was in a boxing match.' I'd do an encore but if he had a late night, he would sleep easily next day.

Our next destination was Amarillo, Texas. Fifty miles from the city we started seeing billboards for a restaurant. THE TEXAS STEAK RANCH – AMARILLO – FREE 72-OUNCE STEAK if you eat it within one hour.

Like thousands before us we had to see this place. 'Heh, Charlie,' I

said, as we passed a stuffed grizzly at the entrance. 'They serve rattlesnakes too...' Charlie was worried enough at the prospect of a seventy-two-ounce steak arriving on his plate but the idea of a snake being slapped down in front of him diminished his appetite more.

The menu arrived and I read it aloud. 'Appetisers... Genuine diamond rattlesnake. By the piece. We warn you now – very little meat, lots of bones. Complaints will get you a live one...'

'I don't want a live snake,' pleaded Charlie.

The waitress took our orders – two ten-ounce Ribeyes, and a Roy Rogers Steak Finger and Wrangler Burger for the kids.

'Side orders?' she asked.

'Onion rings, fries....'

'Beans and salad?'

'Yes.'

'Coleslaw?'

'Why not?'

'Drinks?'

'Four Cokes.'

'Any toppers on your meals?'

'OK... blue cheese.' (America had sautéed mushrooms). This waitress was fast. Did we really need so much?

'Right,' I said to the boys. 'Shall we see what a giant seventy-two-ounce steak looks like?' (There was an example in a case by the bear.) It was so enormous it spilled off a large plate. But to my amazement, you didn't only have to finish the steak within an hour – but all the trimmings too. Baked potato, beans, salad, the works... If you didn't scoff the lot within sixty minutes it cost you fifty dollars. 'How could anyone do that?' asked America.

But 27,560 people had tried. And 4,607 had been successful (1,220 of them women). By the illuminated steak cabinet there was a list of winners. 'They all ate it,' promised the blurb, 'and are eligible for the National Steak-Eating Contest here at the Texas Steak Ranch.'

The victors gave their age, town, time and a comment. Time: 'One hour,' said Peter Friedmann, aged 25, from Zurich, Switzerland.' Comment: 'Vegetarian now.'

Returning to our table, our ten-ouncers had arrived (along with free cowboy hats for the kids). I'd over-ordered. We weren't going to manage all those extras.

The steaks were good but not as good as those at the Cattlemen's

Café. That was the real thing. This was for tourists. When the waitress took our plates, food was still piled on the table. But that didn't stop her sales-pitch. 'OK – four strawberry shortcakes?' I declined the offer.

At Amarillo KOA we met Ken and Wendy Dunn, and Tylor, their two-year-old son. He and Ken were playing baseball.

'I suppose you prefer cricket,' said Ken diplomatically after my boys – given a dozen pitches – had failed to hit the ball.

He and his wife were in the US Airforce and had once been based in Suffolk. 'We had a blast!' said Ken. 'We brought Wendy's folks over and even got her dad used to that warm beer...'

Now they lived in Shreveport, Louisiana. Both worked in maintenance on bombers. Ken said working together helped their relationship. 'It's useful to be able to talk things over in the evening with someone who knows what you're talking about. You don't have to explain acronyms and things...'

Once the kids were in bed I phoned my old friend Charlie, a movie editor who lives in Los Angeles with his American wife, Molly, and two-year-old daughter, Isabella. I hadn't seen him for nearly two years. They were to be our last port of call.

Like most people in the movie industry, Charlie is contracted from film to film. He wasn't working at that moment. 'Great,' I said, brightly. 'Stay unemployed until we leave LA.'

Leaving the shower next morning, I witnessed a striking example of the Americans' dependence on the car. A woman and her teenage daughter, camping only twenty yards away, got in their Chevy and drove to the showers. 'Mah,' said the teenage daughter when they reached it two seconds later, 'I've forgotten my gel. Could you go back and get it for me please.'

Mah dutifully drove to the RV, fetched the daughter's gel and drove back to the showers. Once they were washed, both got in the car and drove the twenty yards to their RV.

Perhaps appropriately, Amarillo is home to a tribute to the automobile. Seven miles west of town on I-40 (the main east-west interstate which replaced legendary Route 66) is Cadillac Ranch where ten battered roadsters stand nose down in the soil (brightly coloured stuff after which the city is named – *Amarillo* is Spanish for yellow). The models, recognisable from their tail fins, date from 1949 to 1963 and were planted by Stanley Marsh III, a millionaire who made his money in helium (the city sits on ninety per cent of the world's supply). Constantly resprayed by passing visitors (encouraged by Mr Marsh), the cars are often used for fashion shoots.

When we arrived we found half-used spray cans littering the ground. The kids grabbed some and I explained carefully how to commit what in normal circumstances would be considered an act of wanton vandalism. But spraying the cars required a certain skill otherwise paint blew back in your face. Once I'd shown the kids they excelled as graffiti artists. Charlie even practised his handwriting. 'Look daddy,' he said proudly, 'I've done a *chuh* for Charles...'

'That's excellent,' I said, sounding like the ultimate liberal parent encouraging a hooligan son, 'Watch me do a *muh* for Matthew...'

We left our mark everywhere: 'Matt, Charles, Nicolai – July 97'. America sprayed the name of her beloved rock group – 'Doctor Explosion. America, Spain'.

For half an hour it was us, the wind and the Cadillacs. Then a gang of teenagers with their own paints arrived, so we hit the road again.

Our morning's work done, we had lunch in an eerie McDonald's. It felt isolated and windswept and eating our burgers with only a handful of other diners, in what felt like nowhere America, I half expected a fully armed nutcase to walk through the door and open fire. But he didn't. We finished our burgers and got back in the RV.

According to an American guide book, Palo Duro Canyon State Park is home to 'one of Texas's best kept secrets – 16,000 acres of jaw-dropping beauty'. We were going to camp there. A warden explained the campground's delights. 'You are gonna love it,' she promised. 'The canyon is the second largest in the country and a lot of folk prefer it to the Grand Canyon itself. It's beautiful with lots of wildlife – racoons, snakes, tarantula spiders...'

'Did she say snakes?' asked Charlie.

'Did she say tarantulas?' said America.

'Oh, they won't hurt you, sweetheart. You'll be in your RV and they don't like campgrounds. Well, you might see racoons, and even a snake, but I doubt you'll see a tarantula...' America sighed in relief. Charlie and Nicolai seemed uncertain.

Palo Duro Canyon State Park was magnificent. The canyon itself – twelve hundred feet from rim to floor – is a million years old and rips through red, yellow and brown rock, some of it two hundred million years old. Our campground, despite being in the middle of such raw nature, had water and electrical hook-ups and only cost twelve dollars a night.

All kinds of activities were available in the park – riding, hiking, fishing, mountain-biking, nature study – but with tarantulas and snakes in their minds, the kids and America settled for a scenic drive first.

That evening we went to *Texas*, a prizewinning musical performed in the park, which celebrates the Lone Star State's history (it was an independent nation from 1836 to 1845). The show unashamedly revels in the rugged Texan spirit and pays homage to the state's size and status. 'Aren't Texans great?' is the message. It's easy to see why it's been playing to packed houses for thirty years. The performance, by eighty amateur singers and dancers on a natural outdoor stage with a six-hundred-foot cliff as a backdrop, is very uplifting – especially if you're a Texan.

During the interval my neighbours in the audience were inspired to speak with pride about their state. 'Yes, sir, Texas is big!' said one. 'I went to Pennsylvania – back in '82 – and I found it amazin' that we could go on tours and visit three states within a few hours. Here you can drive for a day and not leave Texas...'

'Well, I'm a citrus farmer on the Gulf Coast,' said the fellow behind him, 'and it took me thirteen hours to drive up here. Texas is real big, sir! One thousand miles from top to bottom... Eight hundred from east to west...'

The plot was corny and the acting sometimes patchy ('Why do they keep shouting?' asked Charlie – they *were* outside, speaking to a thousand people) but the kids, America and I really enjoyed it – almost as much as the Texans. The setting made it truly sublime and seeing real horses gallop across the scenery was a treat in itself.

The show's finale erupted into a great display of fireworks. Naturally, these were on a massive scale – the bangs louder, the flashes brighter, than anything the kids had ever seen before. Nicolai became terrified, wailing and whining, so I led the nervous boy out. When I tucked him into bed later, he'd forgotten this incident. 'I enjoyed the show, daddy. And I wasn't frightened of the fireworks, was I?'

'No, Nicolai – of course you weren't.' And he went to sleep.

30 A Brush with the Law

While America did some cleaning next morning, the boys and I played in a picnic area and spoke to a woman with two children. She was a doctor, born and raised in Amarillo. And very proud of the fact. 'But you know,' she admitted, 'Amarillo is a place Americans love to mock. Some even call it the nation's most boring city. But we adore our town. It's safe, unpolluted and has awesomely beautiful countryside nearby. We come to the canyon all the time.' She was a fourth-generation Amarillian. 'My great-grandfather left the East in a chuck-wagon and our family's been here ever since...'

She was waiting for her two other kids who were on a GI Joe Camp (kids dress up in army gear and go off into the wilderness with a teacher) and about to return for a tug o' war. As we spoke other parents arrived. A man put some plastic sheets on the ground which I assumed were to stop kids scratching themselves if they got pulled along. But no! Jello (jelly), jam, washing-up liquid and water were thrown down and as the kids played their tug o' war the weaker team was pulled through the mess. Kids got covered in gunk. Everyone found it hilarious. Parental cameras came out, pictures were taken and hoses then turned on for the clean-up. This was where my boys joined in. We trooped back to the RV, soaked, and messed up America's clean floor.

From that moment things spiralled downhill. My sewer tank was full so I stopped at the dump station, connected up my hose and pulled the dumping lever. For a minute the process was smooth. Then (because I hadn't pushed the spongy connector of the sewer hose down far enough) the force of the flow made it jump out of the drain. The hose span around uncontrollably, like a crazed boa constrictor, spraying sludge in every direction – over the ground, over the RV *and* over me. Braving flying pooh, I ran to the lever and stopped the flow. Laughter burst out from the RV. 'Shut up!' I bawled. The kids found the spectacle hilarious. My legs were a mess. I hosed the ground, my feet and the RV. Then I removed my clothes.

Except for my trainers and panama hat, I threw them in a bin and ran Mr Bean-like for a shower. When I returned, clutching my panama to my midriff, America had a towel and clean clothes ready. I dried myself, dressed and we continued our journey.

But fifteen minutes later there was another problem. I dashed into a shop for ice-creams and came out to see America standing stern-faced by the door. 'Two boys want to speak to you,' she said gravely. I looked up to see two teenage boys, leaning against a New Mexico-registered pick-up with 'Amarillo or Bust' sprayed on the rear windscreen. Both looked sheepish. 'Sorry,' said one. 'I wasn't concentrating properly...'

There was a hole in the side of my RV. He'd reversed his pick-up into it. I sighed, bit my lip, smelt his breath to see if he'd been drinking (he hadn't), asked how he could have been so stupid, countered accusations from his friend about my bad parking, then exchanged details. I took photos of the youths, of their pick-up and my damage. Then we shook hands and parted company. A while later, I phoned Cruise America. 'I thought I'd better inform you that a guy reversed into me today...'

'Any damage?' asked the man.

'A hole in a side panel.'

'You call the police?'

'No...'

'Where's the guy who did the damage?'

'No idea – he drove off...'

'He drove *off*? You mean he left the scene of the accident? And you didn't call the police? You gotta get a police report...'

'What, just for a small hole? No one was hurt, we exchanged details and the guy has admitted responsibility...'

'Listen, sir – you have to get a police report for *any* automobile accident. By leaving the scene that guy has committed a felony. He could be in serious trouble...'

I promised to get a police report. First though, I needed a policeman.

It just so happened that at that very moment, less than a mile from Palo Duro Canyon State Park, Trooper Steven Moore of the Texas Highway Patrol had stopped. I saw his parked patrol car and pulled to a halt myself. I got out and told him my story. 'I hope I'm not going over the top grabbing you like this,' I said, 'But they told me I needed a police report...'

'Sir...' said the officer reassuringly, 'you've done exactly the right thing.'

He took down my details. 'This *is* strange,' I said. 'In Britain we tend to think American cops spend their lives chasing killers. I didn't realise a tiny traffic incident could possibly be of interest to you.'

'Well, that's the law, sir. These reports take time but officers check-out accidents in case people change their story later. Unfortunately, some folks are less honest than they should be. Now, this young fella who went into you – he must have known that he was doing wrong by driving off. We'll have a check put out for him.'

'Poor guy,' I thought. 'He's going to be pursued by the Highway Patrol just for a parking-lot accident...'

The heat was fierce so the policeman invited me into his auto-climatised car to complete the rest of the form. Charlie's sorrowful face stared out from the RV. He probably thought he was arresting me. 'Excuse me,' I said. 'Do you mind if I get my son...'

I fetched Charlie, introduced him to the policeman then we got in the car. 'How old's Charlie?' asked the cop. Charlie went mute so I told him he was four.

'You know,' he replied, reflecting. 'I've got a son just turned four – goes by the name o' Rhett...'

'Your name's not Butler, is it?' I asked inanely, trying to add some lightness to the proceedings.

'Excuse me? Oh, no... Moore – Steven Moore.'

He then asked about my rental contract. 'Well, I collected the RV in Orlando at the beginning of June and I'm dropping it in Los Angeles in a month...'

'That's a big trip... Can I look round the vehicle?'

He circled it and inspected the dent but when he went inside my heart sank. Nicolai was sleeping, there was crockery in the sink. I felt like the head of a vagrant family (which of course I was). He looked around, seemingly satisfied, but then asked, 'You and your wife – you're on *vacation* for three months...?'

'Not exactly...' I said, hesitantly. 'I'm writing a book about this trip. America's not my wife. She's an au pair. My wife's at home, working, and I'm writing about a British dad travelling with his kids in America...'

'Sounds great,' he replied, unconvinced.

'Well,' I blathered on, 'Charlie starts school in September. He won't have so much free time for years... My wife's started a new job and works long hours and I just wanted to get them out of childcare, out of polluted London, and give them a wonderful summer...'

'Sounds great...' he said again, this time with more force. 'OK, Mr Collins – you're done. Here's your copy of the report. Have a wonderful trip...'

He got in his car and drove off. I went to the loo, reassured Charlie that everything was fine (daddy definitely *wasn't* going to prison) and started the engine. But just as I was about to pull away, I saw a patrol car in my mirror. It was Trooper Moore. He pulled up behind and walked to my door.

'Mr Collins...' he said. 'You said you were writing a *book* about your trip... Would I be able to obtain a copy?'

Was he asking this because he thought he might be in it? (I *had* taken photographs of him...) Or was he genuinely interested in my trip? 'To be honest,' I said, 'I don't think it's going to be on sale in America. At least not immediately...' (MATC Publishing has not gone transatlantic yet.) 'But I could have you put on the company data-base and send you an order form when it's published... It'll be about twenty dollars,' I added (after mentally calculating how much post and packing might cost).

'That'd be great,' said Trooper Moore. 'I'll look forward to it. I surely will...'

'I tell you what,' I said, suddenly overcome with completely over-the-top enthusiasm for my first potential American customer. 'I've got a copy of another book I did in here somewhere. If I can find it you can take it. But you'll have to send this book back. I know that sounds terrible but it's the only one I've got and it's full of amendments for the next edition. Hang on a second, let me get it...'

I ripped open cupboards and draws until I had it. 'There you go,' I pronounced, triumphantly. '*Matthew's Travels* – hope you enjoy it...'

'That *you*?' asked the policeman, pointing at the cover.

'Sure,' I said. ('Of course, it's me,' I thought. The photo had been taken in the 1980s but kids and a Russian wife surely hadn't aged me *that* much). 'That's me,' I said. 'I had more hair then...'

'Thanks, Mr Collins. I appreciate the gesture. And I look forward to reading this, sir...'

'Good — well, if you could just remember to return it... As I said, it's the only one I've got and the scribbles are for a new edition...' I wrote down the address of Charlie in Los Angeles. 'He's a friend of mine. We'll be with him in a month. If you could send the book there as soon as you've finished it I would be extremely grateful...'

'Don't worry. You have my word. And if there's one thing I have as a police officer, Mr Collins, it's my word... I'll get it back to you, don't you worry, sir...' He gave me his address, in case I needed to contact him.

We shook hands and he went to his car. But then he returned yet again. 'Mr Collins,' he said. 'We normally have little teddy bears to give kids who are traumatised after a car accident. I'm right out of them now, so maybe Charles and Nicolai would like some Highway Patrol stickers...'

'Thank you,' I said. We parted with a handshake.

31 Into New Mexico

We spent that night on a primitive public campground at Lake Meredith, about fifty miles north-east of Amarillo. Our route was now changing. Instead of continuing directly west, we were heading for Colorado.

I'd arranged to stay on a ranch. Having already enjoyed an American ranch holiday, I'd longed to have one with the children. Before leaving home I'd made arrangements with a specialist company (American Roundup — tel: 01404 881777) and booked a week at a child-friendly place up in the Rocky Mountains National Park.

I'd spotted Lake Meredith while planning our trip on my free map from the Visit USA Association in London (there's no US government tourist office in Britain but this privately funded association gives out a free information pack in return for dialling a premium rate phone line — 0891 600530).

Lake Meredith was marked 'National Recreation Area' and wasn't mentioned in my guidebooks but even though it was on the wrong side of Amarillo for Colorado, curiosity compelled me to go there. When I reached the lake and saw a man measuring rocks I asked him about camping facilities. 'You got two choices,' he said. 'None's got hook-ups but there ain't no charge either. The first's at Harbour Bay — you wanna avoid that because it's full of drunks. The second's at Cedar Canyon — that's dry. No alcohol allowed at all ... Can't even drink your own beer. But it's probably your best bet with kids ...'

'Thanks,' I said. These were two stark choices. Before pulling away I asked him what he was up to with the rocks.

'I'm a geologist,' he said. 'They got some great formations here ...'

At Cedar Canyon a small group of RVs were settled on the shore of the lake. I spoke to the owners, reversed on to the sand and squeezed into a gap between two of them.

Dusk was falling and there was a happy, twilight atmosphere on the small, simple campground — the chirrup of crickets, the laughter of children, the crackle of meat on barbecues. The occupants of the RVs next to us were all related. They lived in Amarillo and came here most weekends. 'Lake Meredith's a man-made lake in a National Recreation Area,' said a guy called Randy. 'You can hunt, fish, go boating, jet-ski here – basically do what you want. But you can't *drink*. If you're caught with booze, you're in trouble. But the other campground's crawling with drunks so we don't mind too much...'

To their delight, Randy let the boys sit on his jet-ski. Then they played tag with the other children. They went to bed late. I turned in at one a.m. and left the group sitting on their deckchairs by a fire – laughing and talking, knocking back cans of Coke and Sprite.

The route I had chosen went through a corner of New Mexico on small but very pretty roads. On Route 152 in north-west Texas I stopped at a liquid-propane depot. I'd been running low and as propane powered the fridge, water-heater and oven, thought it was worth filling up. A denim-clad hulk in a stetson, who must have been sixty-five, approached. 'I need to fill up,' I said, clutching my Cruise America handbook. 'I haven't done it before so I'm not sure what to do...' While I fumbled through the handbook (searching for the 'Propane System' section) he connected a pipe to the RV. By the time I'd read the advice to *turn off the propane tank before refuelling* the man was disconnecting his pipe. 'Did you turn off the system before filling up?' I enquired.

'Don't think so,' he replied, smirking. 'But we got there, didn't we? We're all still here – we survived...'

I paid and drove towards the gates before checking directions with another jeans-clad hulk. He was at least sixty too but had the muscular vigour of a man twenty-five-plus years younger. (Or maybe he was only thirty and badly worn.) Whatever, these guys were huge and oozed machismo. And they looked you in the eye and spoke loud. Not for the first time on this trip, I felt small, quiet and self-consciously British. 'Yeh, stay on 87 all through New Mexico,' he said. And spat – a long saliva squirt on to the burning tarmac. 'It's beautiful up there but desolated...' He spat again – another foul but rather expert gob. 'I lived in New Mexico years ago – fifty-seven miles from the nearest town. It was hell when you had to go in twice a day...'

'So, to go up to Colorado?' I continued.

He expectorated again – a beautifully executed turn-of-the-head spin. No doubt, it aided his concentration. 'OK... Turn off north on I-25 and that'll take you all the way to Colorado Springs...'

'Thanks,' I said.

'Sure...' One more final, little flob.

'He was rather disgusting, wasn't he?' squeaked Charlie, sounding like Little Lord Fauntleroy (hardly appropriate in Texas).

'Americans spit,' added Nicolai, prissily. 'We don't spit, do we Charles?'

TTHBTTOOH

GAS

The scenery in the tiny corner of New Mexico we saw lived up to the description on car registration plates ('New Mexico – Land of Enchantment'). It was desolate and parched but the sharp sun and soft natural colours made it look truly enchanting.

En route we stopped at a small supermarket. A luscious-looking woman out of *Viva Zapata* rang up my goods at the cash desk. 'Where y'all from?' she asked.

'England and Spain,' I said.

'Do you speak Spanish?' asked America.

'I wish...' said the luscious Latino. 'I can only speak English...'

We spent that night at Pueblo KOA in Southern Colorado. It had several permanent residents, including Tom from Alabama, a fifteen-year-old who hung around our RV talking non-stop. He told us his stepdad was English and worked on the railroads with his mum. They did eight to twelve-hour shifts and left him in charge of his ten-year-old sister (whom we never saw). 'They work with the conductors,' he said. 'Conductors make real good money – about twenty thousand dollars a week. Or is it two thousand? I dunno but they make a lot. They've been to college and all that...'

After I'd finally persuaded Tom that my boys had to go to bed, and therefore he had to leave, we received another visitor. I opened the door to find a goofy-looking man, about fifty years old, wearing nylon shorts (pulled too high up his crutch) and a tiny white T-shirt several sizes too small. 'Excuse me, sir,' he said. 'May I give your children a soft toy?'

'What?'

'Well, I play a lot of crane-grabbing games in Safeway. You know the thing – you put money in a machine and grab toys with a crane. I'm kinda good at them so I win prizes all the time. This is the biggest thing I've ever won...' And he held up his trophy – a large, ugly, stuffed, chimpanzee. 'I was real lucky with that one – I just managed to grab it by the ribbon... But as I was sayin' – I win toys all the time so my wife makes me give them to kids... Only when the parents are there, of course... It's just that I got so many...' And he pulled more toys from a bag.

The boys eyed them eagerly. 'OK,' I said. You can give them a toy...'

Charlie chose Winnie the Pooh. Nicolai grabbed a small gorilla. 'Well, I better go now,' said the man. 'I promised some little girls a toy...'

'Thanks,' I said and shut the door.

'He was a nice man, wasn't he?' said Charlie.

'I suppose so,' I said. 'But it's not normal for a strange man to give toys to children. You, Charlie – and you, Nicolai – must never, ever, take toys or sweets off anybody you don't know if mummy, daddy or America isn't there. Do you understand?'

'We understand,' they said. And the boys went to bed.

32 Lost Valley Ranch

Next morning I rang the ranch for directions. I knew it was isolated but *not* that it was nine miles from the nearest real road. Insurance warnings rang in my ears. 'Will my RV be OK?' I asked. 'The underneath of the vehicle's not insured.'

'Sure,' replied the woman. 'Bob Foster Junior (the owner) drives one and he's never had a problem. You go nine miles up a dirt road but it's not that bad – just as long as it doesn't rain...'

Within an hour of leaving Pueblo, the heavens opened. Thunder roared. Lightning flashed. Rain lashed the windscreen so ferociously that I had to stop in a Rest Center. Even after the storm had subsided, visibility remained poor and I missed a turning at Colorado Springs. (That's my excuse anyway.)

I drove to a place called Sedalia and followed signs to Deckers (the ranch's nearest village) twenty-eight miles further on. To my horror, the real road soon ran out. I had to negotiate asphalt-less twists, often at horrifically steep gradients. As the engine whirred I watched my fuel gauge plummet. In stretches, I reckon, I was getting three miles to the gallon. When I finally reached Deckers, after some terrifying ascents, I pulled in at a small local store to ask about the nearest gas station.

Friendliness wasn't my first impression here. ALL SHOPLIFTERS WILL BE BEATEN TO DEATH said a prominently-displayed sign. 'Excuse me,' I asked inoffensively (anxious not to upset the old battle-axe at the cash desk), 'is there a gas station nearby?'

'Eighteen miles away,' she grunted. 'Nothing round this way at all...'

'OK,' I said, my heart sinking. 'Thanks...' And I took some liquorice laces for the boys.

We still had twelve miles to go – and nine more of dirt road. I wasn't sure we would make it.

I drove out of Deckers and on to a track towards the ranch. The surface was stony and wet. I had forty-five minutes of slip-sliding, bump-crunching, nail-biting hell. Amazingly, we then reached Lost Valley. I unbelted the boys and we left our tired, mud-spattered motorhome. It looked like it had been through a war zone.

'How're y'all doin'?' 'Great to have you here.' 'Really glad you're staying at Lost Valley.' Fresh-faced young workers each beamed a welcome.

'Do you have a gas supply?' I enquired nervously to the sweet-faced receptionist before I even thought of checking-in.

'Sure.'

'Great!' I said. 'How much is it, please?' (I didn't care if it was ten bucks a pint).

'One thirty a gallon – something like that.'

'Baby, you are beautiful! How wonderful life is! I love Lost Valley already...'

'Would you like to check-in now?'

'Yes, please...' I said, resuming consciousness.

I filled out registration forms and the receptionist asked if I wanted to drive up to my cabin. 'Is it far to walk?' I enquired.

'It's kinda far with kids and bags and things. It's the highest cabin on the ranch.'

'Great... I'll walk.' (I couldn't bear the thought of running out of gas halfway up.)

'Listen, we could put y'all in a pick-up if you like, and have you taken there...'

'Heh, boys – you want to ride in a pick-up truck?'

'Yehhh...!' said the boys. So we went to our cabin in the pick-up truck.

'Daddy,' asked Charlie once we'd reached it. 'Can we buy a pick-up when we get home?'

'Yes, we want a hiccup,' added Nicolai.

'I'll think about it,' I said. (Having never owned a car, I doubt my first will be a pick-up.)

'Colorado's citizens are proud of their state's thin air,' said a guidebook, 'In which golf balls fly further, eggs take longer to cook and visitors tend to lose their breath just getting out of bed...' That must have been why I felt dozy. The ranch was at seven thousand five hundred feet. I was reading the book on my comfy king-size bed. America had the other – the kids were to alternate between us each night. They were out for the count. I had to rouse them for supper.

131

But it was worth rousing them for. Beef Steamboat was the dish of the day but the buffet tables groaned (nay, screamed) with food. Even before our weeks of budget specials, none of us was used to such a spread. Everything was home-cooked and fresh. We burped and belched our way back to our cabin. And then all went to bed.

One of the attractions of a holiday at Lost Valley is the fulltime childcare facility. The ranch brochure promises 're-creation' as well as 'recreation' for the whole family. But having been with my kids so much, I felt like an Italian mama when it came to handing them over to the childminder next morning. It was hard letting go.

There were two other under sixes (older children were allowed to go off riding) – Woody, four, and Spencer, five. 'Are you Marks and Spencer?' asked Charlie.

'My – what accents!' said Woody's mum. 'Can you boys teach Woody to speak right...?'

Charlie and Nicolai seemed happy to let *me* go, so I went to find myself a horse.

The corral was full of cool-looking wranglers – actually college students, mostly only here for the summer. But in Wrangler jeans, cowboy boots, stetsons, checked shirts and neckerchiefs, they all had the gear and looked the part. I felt a right British prat.

I didn't have boots – just a pair of trainers (size thirteen, still embarrassingly huge and white – although nothing a bit of horse pooh wouldn't change). I didn't have a stetson – just a battered panama. I had Levis instead of Wranglers and T-shirts instead of checked shirts. But at least I could ride a bit. Some guests, dressed up like John Wayne himself, had never even been on a horse.

'You say you've ridden before, Matt?' asked Lost Valley's chief wrangler, Brad. 'Well, you're gonna be an expert by the time you leave here.' I looked forward to fulfilment of his promise.

We were divided into groups. I went with the intermediates but when my horse was brought over my heart sank. He was the ugliest brute I'd ever seen. 'Meet Navajo Joe, Matt,' said Dace, the group wrangler. 'He's not exactly pretty but he's smart...'

He certainly wasn't pretty. With his grey-dappled skin, steaming, dribbling mouth, thick fleshy neck and pink bloodshot eyes tinged with revolting yellow gunk, he certainly wasn't going to win any equine beauty contests. But his great personality shone through.

He was gentle, obedient and probably the most responsive horse

I've ever ridden. Amazingly for a mount used by so many different riders, he responded to noises and verbal commands – a click for a trot, a kiss for a canter (or 'lope', as the wranglers called it). An 'easy' then a 'wooohhh' to make him stop. Navajo Joe, I later learnt, was a well-loved Lost Valley 'character' – not impartial to jumping a few fences and escaping to the ranch swimming pool, whenever the fancy took him. On more than one occasion he'd been discovered enjoying a midnight dip.

There were ten in my group – all Americans except for Nigel and Sheila, two Brits now Canadian citizens. Halfway up a mountain Nigel, an oil-industry executive, quietly revealed a secret to me. 'Actually, Matthew, it's not the kind of thing an oil man should boast about but I'm wearing womens' tights – under my jeans. A friend said they would stop my legs chafing...'

Dace had a deal whereby anyone whose hat came off had to buy him a shake. Mine bit the dust pretty soon. 'You'll have to get a string for it, Matt,' he said. 'Although I'm not sure you can get them for panamas...' You also had to buy a shake if you made an *involuntary dismount*. What a euphemism that was. Nobody *fell* from their horse that day.

We had a glorious first morning's ride – trotting, loping and savouring the scenery. I'd never glimpsed so much space – we had twenty-six thousand acres of Pike's Peak National Forest to ride in. After tying up our horses, back at the corral, Nigel checked his tights. I skipped away to my boys.

They'd had a great morning too. Having already used various forms of childcare (a nursery, au pairs, my mother) there are certain things I expect a childminder to do – read the kids a story, give them toys to play with, help them paint or draw. Teaching the art of fly fishing was not on the list. Nevertheless, Kim, the childminder, had been doing precisely that. The children had no hooks but the creek and rods were real. All of them looked skilled enough to join a royal party for the next salmon fishing trip to Scotland.

Although childcare was available for the whole day we swam together then rested that afternoon. After supper, there was a potentially cringe-making, get-to-know-your-fellow-guests session. As an ice-breaker, each member of a family group had to tell a travel story or review their book of the year.

The 'Good Book' was many guests' best read – but most squeezed in a second favourite too. I told a travel anecdote but one man had no story nor book. 'Hi,' he said, 'my name's George. I'm from Alabama. And I guess I'm a man of the '90s. I've got two sons. Both went to college. One came back with a degree and a wife. The other came back with a baby. No degree. No wife...' Everyone took to George immediately.

At the end of the week George made an offer for two horses. (I found that amazing – if some guests liked their mounts, they bought them and had them shipped home.) 'So, you're buying two horses, George,' I enquired, nosily. 'Do you have a farm?'

'Yes, Matt,' he said, 'I'm a cattle farmer...'

'Is cattle farming fruitful?'

'It's not great, Matt. But to be honest – I've been blessed by the Lord...'

'Why is that, George?'

'My folks started Coca Cola in Alabama. I'm one of the people with the rights to it...'

George wasn't the only wealthy guest at the ranch. 'I'm sure we're among the few people here who aren't millionaires,' said Sheila, wife of Nigel, the tights-wearing oil-executive. (Actually, I knew that that wasn't true – as well as the lawyers and business-people, there was also a sprinkling who made this family holiday a financial priority.)

The rides got better each day. And the food stayed superb – copious, filling breakfasts (pancakes, waffles, fries, cereals, fruit, muffins...); giant juicy steaks; perfect barbecues; wonderful buffets; fat *fajitas*; delicious salmon; turkey with cranberry sauce... One lunchtime the children had their first peanut butter and jelly (jam) sandwich. Charlie took a bite and spread jam around his mouth. 'Heh!' said a guest called Polly, 'their first peanut butter and jelly sandwich – this is a Kodak moment...' She snapped a picture of the boys with their sarnies.

Each table had two waitresses. One of ours was Chelsea, a smiley, chatty, happy Californian. Before every meal, she asked the same question. 'OK, you guys, what would you like to drink today? We've got fruit punch, milk, mineral water, iced-tea, coffee, Coke, Sprite, juice... What are you having?' She smiled and patiently waited for our response.

During this trip both boys had become obsessed with diet drinks. I'd explained what they were. 'Diet Coke, please,' requested Nicolai.

'Choose something else,' I ordered. 'That's not for you.'

Chelsea beamed a grin. Charlie then began an explanation. 'No, you can't have Diet Coke, Nicolai,' he said, pompously. 'Diet Coke's for people who need to go on a diet because they're fat. We can't have Diet Coke because we're boys but Chelsea can have it because she's a grown-up. And because she's fat. And because *she* needs to go on a diet...'

Chelsea's smile vanished. And so did Chelsea. Without waiting to hear what the rest of us wanted she ran into the kitchen to phone her analyst. Actually, that's not true. She ran into the kitchen to compose herself. She returned minutes later to take our orders (and an apology from me).

Our other waitress was Nicky. She was tall and blonde and in her Western clothes looked like a character from *Annie Get Your Gun*. Every time she served us, I feared a song. One lunchtime Charlie asked: 'Nicky, are you American?'

'*Very much so!*' she replied.

Charlie caused more confusion at a barbecue. Having covered his face in ketchup he asked me to wipe it. 'Fetch a serviette and I'll clean you up,' I said.

He ran to the wranglers serving food. 'Hello. Have you got any serviettes?'

'Excuse me?' replied a wrangler.

'Have you got any serviettes?'

'What's that?' he asked.

'Ser—viettes...' he repeated.

'No, we ain't got those, Charles...' I found some serviettes myself and as I cleaned his face, the wrangler bounded over.

'Gee — I'm sorry. I didn't know he was after the *napkins*. I thought he was after the *Soh—viets!*'(I didn't tell him the boys were half Russian.)

Like most of the Wranglers (Brad, Bob, Dace, Lee, Dan, Bruce...) the horses had very American names — Slick, Big Mac, Geronimo, Patriot, Santa Fé, Hank, Rebel, Boone, Bear, Moose, Flash, Doc, Winchester, Elvis, Nugget, Calamity, Cactus, Motown, Cindy, Gump, Scooby. And more... You wouldn't have found these in a Sussex riding school. Not surprisingly, Windy and Stinky amused my two most. 'Why is he called Windy?' asked Charlie. 'Is it because he does lots of windy-pops?'

'And why is that one Stinky? Does the person riding him get stinky?' More giggles and titters from them both.

Although only over-sixes were allowed to ride in the groups, small children could ride a horse called Flicka. But only in the corral and supervised by a parent. Flicka was the wisest, gentlest horse I've ever met. 'She's seen every rabbit, every tree, every rock around here,' said Bob Foster Junior. 'She's not surprised by anything...'

Nicolai wanted to run before he could walk. 'Gallop! Gallop! Gallop!' he ordered (thankfully to no avail). Charlie rode Flicka too. At home he's so nervous of animals he gets freaked out by Ozzie, my parents' budgie. Here he had no fear of sturdy quarter horses (the beautiful, mild-mannered beasts favoured by American working ranches).

The boys even learnt some equine biology. One morning, when a stallion was put in the corral I said they couldn't ride Flicka. Charlie responded knowingly, 'Yes, you must be careful with stallions because if you're on a lady horse the stallion likes to chase her to talk to her...'

Their only bad experience was the barn dance. This was led by Spike and his wife Meg. If Olivia Newton-John had had a granny in *Grease*, Meg would have played the part. She wore a red dress, white shoes, had thin legs and hair that looked like it had a million volts through it. Spike ordered the dancers to twirl around their partners. My boys absolutely detested it. Girls tried to grab them and when Nicolai bashed one I removed him from the floor. The barn dance ended with a number Spike dramatically announced that he'd picked up during a trip to England. I waited expectantly... *The Birdie Song* came on.

America wasn't happy that night. She'd run out of cigarettes and put in an order (for when the truck next went to town) but had been told they'd be forty-eight hours.

Cigarettes weren't the only items unavailable at Lost Valley. You couldn't buy alcohol, so groups of secret drinkers formed in cabins. It wasn't long before I was invited over by neighbours, Mike and Laurie, who'd arrived with supplies. Rendez-vous at their cabin became a regular fixture and as Mike mixed margaritas (always apologising for not having a blender) we felt like teenagers in the bike shed.

After only a couple of days the kids were more relaxed than I had ever seen them. Whereas at home we visit parks for greenery, during this trip they'd had the space to run, run, run. They used so much energy they napped in the afternoon and slept until after eight each morning.

But the greatest luxury for me was the riding. It was extraordinary never having to worry about roads. Trees were the only obstacles and before our first big 'lope', Brad warned us all to duck for branches. I stuffed my panama safely up my T-shirt and clicked Navajo Joe into action; but one guy returned, hatless, with gashes down his face.

The strangest sight for me was the children's group. Tiny mounted figures headed for the mountains wearing only stetsons for protection. Not one guest bothered with a helmet. Although Americans are famously litigious it seemed that the right to ride in a cowboy hat, was so strongly enshrined in national consciousness, that this superseded any risk — even if your six-year-old child was astride a fully grown horse. All around the corral were plainly worded signs. 'Colorado Law States That No Equine Professional Can Be Liable For Accidents'. Bob Foster had never faced a court threat (but from summer 1998 would supply hard hats for children).

As the week progressed the rides got even better — longer, faster, more adventurous (and had I not been such an Italian mama, unable to leave my kids all day with Kim — they did need their naps after all — I would have done an all-day cattle round-up). One morning, near a mountaintop, Kelly, the glamorous, nineteen-year-old daughter of Mike, a former US Navy reconnaissance pilot, asked if she could take my picture. 'Sure,' I said, flattered and posed beside Navajo Joe.

'You know, Matthew,' she said, 'I just *gotta* show you to my friends ...'

I sighed modestly.

'This is so neat.'

'Yup.'

'You look *so* much like Mr Bean ...

No one had told me that before. But when I mentioned that we'd once seen Rowan Atkinson driving around London with his son (whom Charlie called Baby Bean) my interest quota rose again.

The final day of the week arrived fast. There was a six a.m. ride to a place called Stag Rock and in the afternoon the Lost Valley Guests' Rodeo was held. Navajo Joe was accidentally unsaddled so I rode

Sparky instead (and came fourth in equine musical chairs).

On our final morning we overslept and missed breakfast. I packed our things, settled my bill and said farewell to Bob Foster Junior. 'So you're heading further west? Did you have a good breakfast, boys?' he asked.

'No,' said Charlie.

'Yes, you did,' said Bob. 'What did you have? Links (American sausages)? Cereal? Orange juice? Fruit?'

'No,' said Charlie again. 'We didn't have anything...'

'Of course, you did,' said Bob, patting him on the head. 'You're getting a memory problem, Charles...' I said nothing. We walked to the RV.

It had been a fantastic week but some aspects wouldn't suit everyone — the Christian atmosphere was occasionally overwhelming and the homely 1950s style and traditional division of labour greatly irritated America. Even Charlie asked 'Why are there no cowgirls? And why don't any of the boys work as waiters?' But the polite, smiling young people (hand-picked from hundreds who apply every year) were definitely an asset for most guests.

'You know,' said Dick du Bose, husband of ('Kodak Moment') Polly, 'these kids are an inspiration. When I was their age I wanted to drink whisky and raise hell...'

The wicked side of me sometimes wished that this lot could have raised hell as well — instead of being so *nice*.

But reality returned soon enough. We left the nine-mile dirt road and halfway to Deckers an overtaking driver wound down his window to bawl at me. 'Move over asshole!' he yelled as he stuck a finger up. We were now back in the real world.

33 Back on the Road

Back in Deckers a group of bikers stood in front of the little, local store. Further down the road at Woodland Park more bikers were parked at a gas station. They were a mixed bunch — aged twenty-five to fifty but all dressed the same in black leathers and bandannas or skull caps. None wore a helmet.

After filling up, I asked a bunch from the 'Minnesota Chapter' if I could take a picture of the kids by their bikes. 'Sure,' they said, open and welcoming. Two lifted Charlie and Nicolai on to a multi-coloured Harley Davidson. 'You British, huh? We know some bikers from Wey–bridge in Surrey. You ever heard of that town?'

'Oh yes,' I said. ('They must be up-market Hell's Angels,' I thought).

This lot were on their way to a meeting in Sturgis, South Dakota. A quarter of a million bikers were expected that weekend.

We didn't drive far. I'd been tempted to visit the *North Pole – Home Of Santa's Workshop* but drove to the entrance at the foot of Pike's Peak to find yet another pricey theme park. Not long afterwards, I checked into Buena Vista KOA. The campground lived up to its name — there was a great view of the Rocky Mountains.

Coming out of the registration office I met a woman in her seventies. She looked like one of those old dears I see in Safeway on Monday mornings. But instead of a shopping trolley, this babe had a 750 Yamaha. She sat astride it proudly, dressed in blue Levis, black biker's boots and a well-worn, red leather jacket. The raised visor of a stars and stripes open-faced helmet let me see her twinkling, wrinkled face. She reminded me of a character in a 1970s cartoon TV commercial — the old lady from Trebors Refreshers. 'Ride on, granny – it's the fizz that gives you whiz...'

Her seventy-something husband, whose identical silver Yamaha was propped up next to hers, emerged from the office, his black leather jacket blowing open. Revealed were the contours of his big, bouncing belly and a NUMBER 1: JESUS badge, sewn on to a tight, white shirt. 'How yah doin', bud?' he asked, taking my hand.

They were from Lubbock in Texas and also *en route* to the bikers' meet in Sturgis — a two-thousand-mile round trip ride. The husband produced a tent from his pannier. 'Where d'yah want it, Martha?' he asked.

'Anywhere, honey. Just not far from the rest rooms... And not so close to other tents that you trip over guy-ropes when you go for your pees in the night...'

Only minutes later, he had erected the tent. I was impressed. 'Well we've been camping and biking since the 1940s,' he said. 'We ain't gonna stop until we die...'

To my astonishment it turned out the woman was originally from Great Yarmouth. 'I was a war bride,' she boasted in an accent with a discernible Norfolk whiff. 'And Jim just swept me off my feet. I was nineteen-years-old when I arrived in America. I don't think I'd have ever got into motorcycling and camping if I had stayed at home in Yarmouth...'

The KOA's play area was well-equipped. It even had a mini assault course. The campground was sandy, flat and almost treeless, which meant it was easy to watch the children from the RV. They soon met two girls – Georgia and Kimberley from Oklahoma City, who were touring in a RV and a Jeep. 'Dad drives the motorhome and mum drives behind,' informed Georgia. She asked if we were there for the 'Jeep Jamboree'.

I said we didn't have a car, adding that I didn't even own one in *England*. Kimberley found this unbelievable. Georgia said that thousands of Jeeps had gathered in Aspen. She ran to her RV to show me the souvenirs she had collected – Jeep badges, coolers, a cap and a rucksack.

The girls helped the boys on the assault course. But they had trouble tackling it themselves. Both were *very* overweight. I asked their age.

'Twelve,' said Georgia.

'Thirteen,' said Kimberley. 'We're six months apart...'

'We're stepsisters,' informed Georgia. 'My dad's not my real dad. And *my* mum's not *her* real mum. My real mum married her real dad... And her real mum married my real dad – although they've both split up now...'

'Do you still see your real dad?' I asked.

'Not much,' answered Georgia. 'He's got a new family and he's real busy so he doesn't have much time for me... And she don't see her real mum now much either...'

The girls invited us back to their RV where the real/unreal mum and dad were making a fire. Soon we were all toasting smores.

Later, when the kids were in bed, Georgia knocked at the door. 'We going home tomorrow,' she said. 'So we thought you might like these...' She gave me some Hershey's chocolate, a box of Honey

Grahams (biscuits) and a giant bag of 'jet-puffed' marshmallows. America and I stuffed them. We soon felt jet-puffed ourselves.

This was going to be our first Colorado night in the RV. The evening was cool and the over-cab bunk a contrast with the ranch's king-size bed and soft quilt.

As it got later the temperature dropped dramatically. By midnight I was frozen and shivering. Having come to hate my ancient, stinking, feather-leaking, sleeping bag (In 1992 I'd washed it in a Walthamstow launderette and ruined it in the tumble drier) I had had Khelga take the offending object home. (It was built to Everest-expedition standards so was inappropriate for the Southern States, anyway.) Since then, I'd slept under a single sheet – until now, fine. But Colorado nights would prove different.

I ransacked the cupboards, looking for towels, and soon accumulated six. I climbed up to the bunk, put on two T-shirts, a pair of jeans and socks, and pulled Charlie and Nicolai close to me. Then I unzipped their *101 Dalmatians* sleeping bags and tried to wrap the two around us all. But as they were only four-feet-six long my feet protruded from the bottom. I rezipped their sleeping bags and made do with towels. I woke up at six a.m. shivering again. I would have to invest in a sleeping bag.

After breakfast, at which the boys gleefully imitated Chelsea, our ranch waitress ('OK, you guys... What would you like to drink? We've got fruit punch, iced-tea, orange juice, hot chocolate...' Actually we only had water), we drove to Durango following a route suggested by Bob Foster Junior.

This used the lowest possible mileage. I'd begun to worry about exceeding my allowance. With Cruise America, they calculate the distance of your chosen route (by feeding your details into a computer) before you book your RV. You then buy mileage in five-hundred-mile 'packs'. If you exceed it, you settle at more than the upfront price.

I'd bought five thousand five hundred miles which I'd assumed would be ample – even allowing for diversions. But having missed exits, taken wrong turnings and got lost several times (as well as using the RV like a car for shopping and sightseeing), I was approaching my limit and had at least twelve hundred miles to cover before Los Angeles.

At least the scenery was exquisite – Alpine, almost Swiss

(although the Rockies looked bolder, more majestic). The first sign that the end of our trip was approaching appeared in the form of occasional Californian car number plates. I was tempted to slow down and spin out the remaining distance for as long as possible. But I had deadlines – for the RV return and our flight.

I pushed on but the radio drove me potty. For miles, the only accessible stations were fundamentalist Christian or country music-based. I couldn't bear them. It was either hell and brimstone or endless redneck bleating and twanging. But then I found a rock 'n' roll station. I felt sane again. Until commercial breaks ruined everything...

Belatedly, I was wishing I'd brought some cassettes. I should have realised they'd be useful on a five thousand five hundred mile drive. I was now reduced to America's tapes of 1960s British music or a 1990s Spanish mod group, Los Flechatos (The Little Arrows). They soon drove me potty too.

But then she produced a winner. Rooting around in her trusty rucksack she came up with something I adored – *Ricks Road* by Texas, the female-led British band. They had a great driving tune – *So In Love With You*. With the volume on maximum and the kids protesting pointlessly ('Turn it down! Down! You crazy man...!') I set the cruise control at fifty-five mph and sailed through south-west Colorado.

34 The Tin Cup Café

Just before Del Norte, an unassuming town, I overtook a slow-moving trash cart. COYOTE'S THE NAME – TRASH IS THE GAME, said the logo on the side. It reminded me of a London skip company's proud claim: OUR BUSINESS IS CRAP.

At Del Norte we stopped at The Tin Cup Café. This was a bad choice. A handwritten notice was pinned to the door: PARENTS – PLEASE KEEP YOUR CHILDREN SEATED AND CONTROLLED AT <u>ALL</u> TIMES. CUSTOMERS DESERVE THIS COURTESY. THANK YOU.

We opened the door and Charlie tripped, landing on his face as we entered. Customers turned and stared.

The Tin Cup clientele looked like it hadn't changed in decades. Three women with beehives sat at one table; a bearded old boy sporting a sailor's cap, accompanied by a man in a stetson, shared another. Three elderly construction workers in checked-shirts and baseball caps muttered over coffee in a corner. And an overweight, grown-up family of five sat by the table we took. Almost every customer smoked. There was a nicotine haze in the air. Mine were the only children present.

Aphorisms, handwritten on scruffy bits of paper and stuck to the walls, were everywhere: 'Life Is Uncertain – So Eat Your Desert First'; 'The Food's So Good That Even The Chef Eats Here...'

The waitress, a woman with the lankest, greasiest hair I'd ever seen, approached, extremely po-faced. I asked her if it was OK just to drink. 'So what d'yah wanna drink?' she replied.

'Four hot chocolates, please.'

As she turned round I noticed another aphorism: 'Mom's Rules – Wipe Your Feet, Sit Up Straight, Don't Talk With Your Mouth Full.'

'Look,' exclaimed Nicolai. 'This wall is pink!' (Actually, it was very faded orange.)

While our order was made up I visited the loo. There was an illustrated map of the US by the door. 'America – Home Of The Brave. The Government Of The People By The People Shall Not

Perish From The Earth.'

When I returned the drinks had arrived. Each was a DIY job. There were four packs of chocolate powder, four mugs and four pots of water. The water in my pot was tepid. 'Excuse me,' I ventured to the greasy-haired waitress. 'I'm afraid mine's not hot.'

'I'll put it in the microwave,' said Greasy.

We drank our hot chocolates as though in a church. America and I spoke in hushed tones. The boys even stayed subdued too. But then, in a flash, Nicolai grabbed the salt, removed the top and emptied it into his mug. He put the cup to his lips, took a gulp and spat a mouthful out. 'Ugh! That's disgusting! I hate it! Daddy, that's disgusting hot chocolate!'

All eyes trained on us. Greasy hurried over. 'Anything the matter?' Her tone was contemptuous. 'He don't like his hot chocolate either?'

'No, he's fine...'

'I'm not fine,' interrupted Nicolai. 'It's disgusting! I hate it!'

'He's fine,' I repeated. 'I'm afraid he put some salt in his cup... Now, of course, he doesn't like the taste. It was his fault. I'm sorry... One more hot chocolate, please... Thank you very much...' She retreated, sighing. Her body language said we were scum.

Another DIY kit arrived. She plonked it on the table. Nicolai was placated.

Once we were orderly again America told me about how she and her friends put salt to use at home. 'Sometimes, in summer, you go out with your friends and drink sangria or tequila all night. You get really drunk so before going home you drink salty water to make yourself sick. It's great — you vomit and you're not drunk anymore.'

Spaniards are funny. On the Costas it's tempting to assume that we British top the league for recreational consumption of large quantities of alcohol. We all know the Germans and Scandinavians like a drink but Spaniards often seem happy with a glass of wine, or even a coffee, while we knock back gallons of beer and spirits.

But America wasn't the first to tell me about contemporary, youthful, Spanish drinking habits. Our first au pair, Teresa from Seville, a sensible, hard-working medical student (partial to wearing very short skirts which had Brazilian boys, living in the house opposite, leaping over the wall into our garden uninvited), liked nothing better than to go out and get totally slaughtered whenever she had something to celebrate. And, smiling nostalgically, she recounted stories of Andalusian *fiestas* – begun with the purchase of cheap Spanish whisky (and plastic cups to drink it from) and followed by a trip to some quiet *plaza* to get blotto...

But you rarely see drunk Spaniards on the Costas. We're the ones shamefully causing havoc. Perhaps the locals are too busy making money. Or perhaps they're more reserved in front of foreigners. Whatever, the young ones like a drink.

After America's salt tip, Charlie demanded more hot chocolate.

'No,' I said, firmly. 'We're leaving now ...'

'But that's not fair! Nicolai had two drinks. I only had one ...'

'Yes – but his first one got ruined ...'

'But that was his fault. I wasn't naughty with the salt.'

'Charlie, we're going ...'

'But I want more hot chocolate.'

'No. We are leaving.'

'I'm going to have one.'

'No, you are *not* ...'

I requested the bill. The beehives arose, each placing a dollar bill carefully on the table. One woman put down three quarters – the tip.

'I want a hot chocolate.' He was becoming tiresome.

'You're not having one.'

'Yes, I *am* ...You're horrid.'

'Shut up!'

'Don't you say shut up to me!'

With wonderful timing, Charlie had a tantrum, providing the perfect, final embarrassment – just as po-faced Greasy brought our bill. I left six bucks on the table and got out. Charlie was snivelling – protesting uncontrollably, tears careering down his face. Nicolai walked smugly behind. As I shut the door, customers sighed. We boarded the RV and made for Durango.

Nicolai was indulged that day. Within minutes of leaving, Charlie was asleep. But Nicolai refused to doze off. So America scratched his back. He lay across her lap, purring like a cat. Then she massaged his forehead. Finally he was sleeping too.

On the outskirts of Durango I tuned into the local radio's PBS (public broadcasting service). An *ABC News* bulletin announced that 'England's Queen Mother is ninety-seven today'.

'God Bless her,' I thought. And pulled into Durango East KOA.

35 Starstruck in Mesa Verde

If you ever have the chance to see a rodeo – grab it! We saw our first in Durango, Colorado, a town founded in 1880 as a rail junction for Silverton (a gold-rush community, forty-five miles away) and described by Will Rogers (comedian, journalist and 1920s film star, although probably now best known in Britain as the man who gave his name to the park where George Michael was arrested for 'lewd conduct') as 'Out of the way and glad of it...'

Today it's a tourist spot. Visitors come for the steam trains through the mountains (popular with skiers, bikers and hikers) and to raft on the Animas River. But Durango remains a genuine small town.

This was made clear when I entered the First National Bank. What a contrast this place was with the Nat West, Fulham Broadway. They don't even display a tankard or modest wooden shield for their staff's sporting endeavours. But Durango's First National had trophies on every wall. Not silver though... Stuffed! Taxidermised animal heads were mounted everywhere – moose, reindeer, mountain goat. And above a set of clocks – one complete moose. They gave the bank a special, local feel.

I lifted up Nicolai so he could stroke a goat's head. A woman approached. 'They were all shot by our president,' she said, proudly. 'Mr White... He's a famous hunter. And travels the world for his sport. Would you like to see a brochure about our bank?' She scuttled away to fetch the document – 'The Bank That Built Durango' by Duane A. Smith. 'Commemorating 110 years of service to the people in south-western Colorado.'

I thanked her and queued for a cashier. A woman in front of me held a child in a pouch. 'He can't walk,' stated Nicolai knowingly, 'Because he's a tiny baby.'

'Actually, he's six years old,' said the woman turning round. The creature was no child but a dormant chihuahua. 'He gets tired so I help him.'

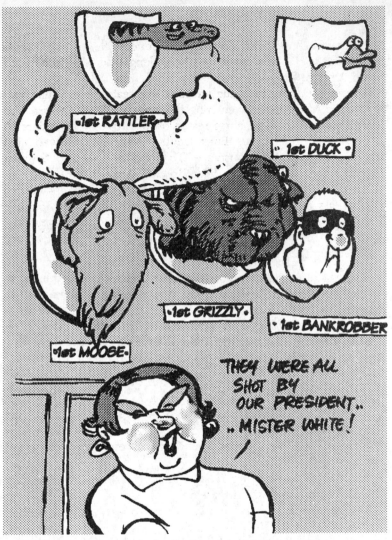

'What a stupid, lazy, little dog!' exclaimed Charlie. 'He's going to get fat like his owner...'

I withdrew some cash on my credit card. Then I scoured town for a cheap sleeping bag. There were plenty of outdoor shops – but all rather pricey. I would have to wait for another Wallmart.

We enjoyed the railway and (noticing a poster) decided on the rodeo – 'Round Eight of the Durango Pro-Rodeo Series presented by

The Durango Pro-Rodeo Company'. I drove to the town outskirts and stuck the RV in a quagmire (the parking field was so boggy I feared it might sink).

After a pre-show barbecue we took our seats. To a triumphant fanfare the MC appeared, entering the arena with the flourish of a Lone Ranger. His white horse reared on cue to another fanfare. A wave of excitement hit us. But a lengthy pre-amble followed. First there were thanks to sponsors — 'To Purgatory Ski and Summer Resort, home of the Alpine Slide; to the *Durango Herald* — your daybreak daily; to the O'Farrell Hat Company — makers of fine quality hats (whether you ride or not...); to the Uté Mountain Casino — where action meets excitement; to Wendy's Hamburgers; to La Plata County Fair...' To endless others... Then there was the usual reassurance:

'Ladies and Gentlemen, you may have heard that riding bulls and broncos at rodeos is wrong. You may have heard that rodeo animals are abused. Ladies and Gentlemen, these animals are cared for and treated well. They are *not* abused. Such claims, ladies and gentlemen are a load of *hot air*...!'

After this came the *Star Spangled Banner*. The audience rose, each member placing hand on heart. Even the caterers clearing up the barbecue stood to attention, looking moved.

But when things finally started they were spectacular. We had front-row seats and as bulls and broncos bucked, we became mud-splattered. The boys adored the action — especially when the cowboys took a tumble.

'Are many injured riding bulls?' I asked the rodeo manager, Jeff Mannix, when I met him afterwards.

'Few,' he told me. 'These guys know how to fall. And bulls are less risky than broncos. Bad injuries happen when a guy's fingers get stuck in a bronco's hand straps and then the thing falls on him...'

The Durango rodeo was small but a great family spectacle. A clown ran on between events (sometimes ducking loose bulls and broncos himself) and entertained kids in the audience. There were also children's competitions — like 'Mutton Bustin', a sheep riding race and the highlight for Nicolai. 'I want to gallop on a sheep,' he said. (Next time we went to the English countryside, he tried — the ewe didn't appreciate his efforts.)

149

Having checked out of the campground that morning, I returned but found it full. 'Last week of the schools' break,' said the owner. 'Everywhere's gonna be busy. Try North Durango or Cortez KOAs...'

I tried Mesa Verde instead. The National Park, once home to the vanished Anasazi tribe and famous for their elaborate cliff dwellings, was on my itinerary anyway. And a guidebook reassured me that the campground there 'never fills up'.

We arrived at eleven p.m. All of us were gasping. (I'd run out of drinks.) Nicolai was crying. He was hot and tired – the kids hadn't slept that day. We drove up a mountain to Mesa Verde village and found a twenty-four-hour gas station and launderette but no open shop or drinks machine.

We continued to the campground. Despite my guidebook's promise I couldn't find a space. I drove round interminably, finally found one, reversed in and turned the engine off.

'Are you going to kill that light?' asked a sudden voice in the dark.

'Sure,' I said, noticing a glow above my door.

'Beause I wouldn't want you to forget about it before you went to bed.'

'Don't worry,' I replied. 'Pompous twat,' I thought. And went inside the motorhome and switched it off.

I rejoined America at the table. She was smoking, inhaling deeply, contentment on her face. I looked at the area where the voice had come from but couldn't see a vehicle or a tent. 'Where is he?' I whispered.

'Sleeping on the ground... Under the stars!'

I looked into the sky. The stars were bright. Thousands were twinkling up above. Suddenly something rustled. A log hit some embers. A silhouette arose and stoked the fire which crackled decisively into life. Smoke blew into our RV – the door and a window were open. 'Excuse me,' I said, aggressively. 'Are you going to have that all night?'

'Sure am,' said the voice. 'That's what we do here in the West of the United States. Sleep under the stars by a fire...'

'Right...' I said. 'It's just that I've got two kids sleeping in the motorhome and I wouldn't want them to die from smoke-poisoning.'

'Oh...' he said, reflecting, less certain. Then, dramatically, his attitude changed. 'No problem. I'll put it out.' He removed the log and killed the embers. 'So...' he uttered sweetly, 'what part of the UK are you from?'

Within only seconds, hostility between us had vanished into the ether. Within one minute we were buddies. 'You know, my wife's from Bristol, but she's asleep in the van. And I got two sons of ten and twelve. They're here with me by the fire.' I looked down to see two giant, purple chrysalises – the boys ensconced in their sleeping bags. 'You want a drink? I'm Rick. Who are you guys?'

'I'm Matthew – from London. And she's America – from Saragossa in Spain.'

'Did you say *America*?' America nodded. 'Now *that* is a beau–ooo–tiful name... I'm from St Petersburg in Florida.'

He fetched us a Coke each. America drank hers, stubbed out another cigarette then retreated.

'Good night, America,' said my new friend. We talked and star-gazed. He pointed out constellations. 'You know, I've spent a lot of time studying astronomy. That's why I wanted your light off. We get so much light pollution in Florida that you can't see them like this. But here... man, you know, it's truly awesome...'

I told him that for generations my family had gone to sea and that my uncle and grandfather could navigate by the stars while I couldn't even recognise a single constellation.

'Well you see that one there – that's the Big Zipper...' He slapped his thighs. 'What *am* I saying? You know, I've just spent an hour talking with some campers about Clinton. Man, I hate that guy... What a creep! But he's gonna pay the price some day. That's ridiculous though... What I meant to say was that's the *Big Dipper*. And just above it, you'll see the North Star. See where I mean?'

I had it. 'That's fantastic...' It was a beautifully clear night. 'But I thought the North Star was the brightest in the sky. I always assumed it was that one...'

'No, sir – that's a planet. Maybe Jupiter or Venus – I can't tell. Heh now, d'yah see that?' And he pointed to a shooting star dancing across the sky.

We explored other constellations, examined the Milky Way, and even discussed the Southern Hemisphere. 'Now if we were in Antarctica we'd see the Southern Cross. That's a beau–ooo–tiful sight...'

Ray lived in St Petersburg and worked for a computer company.

But it had taken him only two days to drive to Colorado from Florida. I was impressed. 'It's taken me over two months...'

'Well, when I drive, Matt,' he boasted, 'I really go for it. We've got a VCR in the van and a whole bunch of videos. So the kids just watch their movies while we drive. We did eleven hundred miles on the first day. Left Tampa around six a.m. and got to St Louis around nine in the evening. We did the rest next day...'

By the time we'd finished talking it was nearly two a.m. Rick crept back to his snoring sons and I went inside to wrap myself in towels. It was another cold night.

" There yer go ! ...Clinton's Comet ! "

36 Purple Hearts and Heaps o' Kids

Mesa Verde (Green Table), a densely wooded plateau, rises from the deserts of south-western Colorado, its flat top greener than the dry lands below. Fourteen hundred years ago, Native American tribes cultivated the area now known as the Mesa Verde National Park and built elaborate cliff dwellings. But around AD1275 (seven hundred years after their ancestors had arrived) the tribes mysteriously disappeared, leaving behind their extraordinary homes.

When the Navajo Indians arrived two hundred years later they named their predecessors the Anasazi — or 'ancient ones'.

Today, Mesa Verde is America's only national park exclusively devoted to archaeological remains. We visited the museum but didn't climb the cliffs — my priority was to buy a sleeping bag.

I drove to the nearest Wallmart and bought their cheapest (at fourteen dollars it was nylon and very nasty). I also bought jeans for the boys (they demanded Wranglers after noticing the cowboy label) and a cowboy belt each. They already had their Texas Steak Ranch stetsons. 'Can we get boots now?' asked Charlie, pushing his luck. 'And a lasso and a gun — go on, daddy...'

I resisted and we continued west. But we only reached Cortez, where I pulled into the campground.

For the first time in weeks we were surrounded by Europeans, many driving Cruise America RVs (the company's based in Phoenix, Arizona).

The boys had a nap. I tidied the motorhome then strolled to the pay phone outside the office. *En route* I passed a pick-up with PURPLE HEART emblazoned on the Texan registration plate. (There was a strong military presence here — two sites before, a Jeep's plate proclaimed: US NAVY RETIRED – SERVED WITH PRIDE.) I was impressed by the Purple Heart. Wasn't that the equivalent of the British VC? A nearby grey-haired figure attended to a barbecue. Was *this very man* the hero?

'Excuse me, sir,' I said. 'May I ask you about your registration plate?'

'Go right ahead.'

'How did you get the Purple Heart?'

'Injured in combat...' (Didn't you have to do more?)

'And... Did you do anything to get injured?'

'No, sir. Just got caught by some Vietnamese APR. Knocked out a load of us. I was one of the lucky ones.'

'So were you badly injured?'

'Bullet in the leg.'

'And does everyone who gets injured receive the Purple Heart?'

'Sure does. That's the decoration for injured soldiers...'

'And do they all display it on their car registration plates?'

'In Texas they do. 'Cause you get a reduction in your annual plate charge. Like, we pay around three bucks instead of seventy.... It's saved me a bit over the years.'

'What a great idea! We don't have that system in Britain...'

'Well, you should...'

'Yes, we should... Thank you, sir.'

'You bet.' And he went back to coating his chicken with spray-on butter.

A couple of days later I saw a Californian-registered motorhome with PEARL HARBOUR SURVIVOR inscribed on the plate. Americans rejoice in their military history more than us. You never see British cars saying I SURVIVED THE BLITZ. If we'd had the same system, every car in London would have said it in the late 1940s.

After talking to the vet I phoned Charlie in LA. 'I can't wait to see you,' I said. 'I'm really looking forward to some grown-up conversation ...'

'Well, don't get your hopes up,' he warned. 'I *have* been in Los Angeles for the last four years...'

The kids slept until early evening. I'd promised them a swim but by the time they were ready it was dusk. We got out of the RV to see the sun setting and a thin, crescent moon in a silver sky.

But people were still in the pool. Charlie and I immersed ourselves while Nicolai posed delicately on the steps. 'Daddy, I need a wee,' he suddenly announced. 'Daddy, I need a wee-wee quickly – now...'

It was warm in the brightly illuminated water and increasingly cold and dark outside. 'Come on, Nicolai, wait a little while. Come into the water and warm up.'

'But, daddy, I need a wee, I really do.'

'Nicolai,' I said, encouragingly. 'Why don't you come into the lovely water?'

'*Because I don't want to do my wee-wee in the swimming pool!*' he yelled. Two bathers stared, disapprovingly.

I strode out of the water, picked him and Charlie up and carried them barefoot across sharp pebbles to the rest room.

'It's nice and warm here,' shouted Nicolai from his locked cubicle. 'Let's stay in this toilet all night.'

I carried them back and we got in the pool. 'Isn't this great?' I said. 'We're having a midnight swim.'

But Nicolai still complained. 'I don't like it here. I want to go in the 'coozi...' I now fancied it too. So we left the pool and lowered ourselves into the bubbling water.

A woman in her forties, a girl of around twenty and a small child were already in it. I assumed there were baby, mother and grandmother. The older woman asked where we were from.

'London, England,' replied Charlie, robotically.

'Wow!' she gasped. 'You are a long way from home.'

'Where are you from?' I asked.

'Salt Lake City...'

'And are you on vacation in Colorado?'

'Colorado and Arizona... We just arrived from the Grand Canyon.'

'And did you ride the Grand Canyon Railway?' (I fancied it as a treat for the kids.)

'Certainly not. That's too expensive for us...'

'No, it's not cheap, is it?... About a hundred and forty dollars for a family of four.'

'Yes. And we're a family of fifteen. So that makes it around three hundred and fifty dollars...'

'You've got thirteen kids?'

'Well, actually I had fourteen. Unfortunately, I lost one five years ago.'

I asked her how old they were. 'Well, Tiffany's twenty-one, Lindy's twenty, Sally's eighteen, Wendy's seventeen, Marty's fifteen, the twins – Timmy and Tammy – are thirteen, Jake is eleven, Martha is nine, Jimmy is seven, Willy is five, Amy is three, and this is Matty – he's twenty months. That's right, isn't it, Tiffany?'

'Nearly, mom... except Jake was twelve last week.'

'Oh, poor Jake. Yeh – he's twelve now...'

She told me they travelled in two thirty-foot motorhomes. 'My husband drives one and I drive the other. Well, we better be leaving. I got the older girls doing dinner.'

The owner then arrived. 'Sorry, folks,' he said, 'but I gotta close things round here...'

'Are you a cowboy?' asked Charlie. (He'd noticed his cowboy boots and chunky belt.)

'Well, I used to be,' he replied. 'But I got too old for breakin' horses. Had forty head in California at one time... But now I work with the KOA...'

'You see, daddy,' said Charlie. 'He *is* a real cowboy.' I picked the boys up and carried them to the RV.

37 Indian Country

We spent our last moments in Colorado at Four Corners – the only US point common to four states, where Colorado meets New Mexico, Arizona and Utah in the Navajo Nation, America's largest Indian reservation.

Four Corners epitomises American attitudes to land – the borders were drawn along lines of longitude and latitude without any regard for natural boundaries. There's not much to see (except desert and Native American souvenir stalls) but tourists get a kick out of crouching down on all fours and putting a limb in each state.

The kids were drawn to a ceremonially dressed warrior and squaw, posing by a tepee with a horse for tourist photographs. I queued up, handed over the kids then a dollar.

After two pictures I requested more. 'Cost you another dollar,' said the warrior. I handed him a buck and took the photo.

'Do you mind if I take others?' (Nicolai refused to smile.)

'One more dollar...' I gave him several bucks and snapped away.

'Thanks,' I said.

'My pleasure,' said the warrior, who then added cheekily: 'Perhaps a little tip?' I handed over a dollar's worth of change. 'Now you have a great day, guys...'

Next in line for pictures were other Native Americans. They were dressed more typically in jeans, T-shirts and trainers.

'Where you all from?' asked the warrior.

'Wyoming – we're Crow.... But I guess *you* grew up here...'

'Actually,' he muttered. 'I'm from Idaho...' (His companion, Latanya, later told me *she* was Navajo).

Our drive would take us through desert. Before leaving Cortez I'd passed a sign: THE NEXT FULL SERVICE TOWN ON THE NAVAJO TRAIL IS 255 MILES.

I'd pulled in at a supermarket, loaded up with supplies (including gallons of water) and, shortly afterwards, stopped at a gas station (at one eighty-eight a gallon, the most expensive so far). From Four Corners we were in Arizona.' Heh, boys,' I said, 'we're in the desert.

'Will we see camels?' asked Charlie.

I diverted north to Monument Valley and clocked the spooky, huge, red rock towers. That wasn't difficult — the sandstone monoliths, familiar from countless Westerns, are visible from US163 for over thirty miles.

Back on US160 we diverted to the Navajo National Monument, site of three Anasazi cliff-dwellings. Unfortunately, the best preserved required a seventeen-mile hike or horseback ride.

One problem travelling with small kids is that they don't give a damn about culture (they're not great hikers either). As we crossed the Navajo Nation all they could talk about was Windy and Stinky, two Lost Valley Ranch horses.

I couldn't tell them any interesting facts I'd learnt. But forgive me while I try some on you:

As late as the 1830s federal policymakers had planned to create a permanent Indian country in the West but in little more than a decade those plans had altered through American expansion.

Indian reservations grew out of the US government's attempts to prevent fighting between Native Americans and whites while encouraging white settlement. Originally conceived to prepare them for assimilation into Anglo-American society, the reservations functioned as wardships for a century. At the beginning of the 1960s, Supreme Court decisions reasserted the tribes' standing as semi-sovereign nations.

The Navajo Nation covers seventeen million acres of north-eastern Arizona, southern Utah and north-western New Mexico. Over a hundred and forty thousand Navajo live here, one tenth of the USA's Native Americans. The nation, the largest in America, has its own police force and laws. Within its boundaries, the smaller Hopi reservation is home to ten thousand people.

The Hopi are renowned for their spiritual, non-materialistic way of life. It would have been wonderful to see a ceremonial Hopi dance (visitors are occasionally welcomed) but the kids really wouldn't have stood for it. I tuned into a local radio station for some Native American music and continued through the desert for two more hours. We arrived at Williams after dark.

38 The Grand Canyon

I'm ashamed to admit that my main reason for visiting was merely because it was *en route*. It's an obvious sight and, having been thoroughly spoilt by all my travelling, I'd seen plenty of those.

But no matter how far you've travelled, no matter how much you've seen, nothing can prepare you for your very first glimpse of America's awesome Grand Canyon. It is sublime. Grab any opportunity to see it. (And if you're fit enough and have the chance to hike in it, jump at that chance like a shot.)

You approach the canyon from the South or North Rim. The South is more accessible and ten times more popular. 'Tourist hell in summer,' one camper had warned me.

We played real 'Johnny Tourists' and took the Grand Canyon Railway. Stories of nose to bumper South Rim traffic jams had discouraged me from driving and besides, the kids were thrilled at the prospect of another steam-train ride. (I'd also been put off by learning of a couple who reversed over the North Rim as they argued over a can of Coke. They got trapped on a ledge and were rescued by helicopter whose team cut their motorhome roof off and winched them to safety from their bed.)

The scenery from the Grand Canyon Railway is not spectacular. But to spice up the journey (two and a half hours each way) there's plenty of on-board entertainment.

The musicians were fabulous; then a bear called Smokey arrived with his Parks Service minder (to remind us of forest-fire hazards) and posed for photographs with the boys. By the time he left they were great buddies.

But half an hour later, outside the rest room, we found a sweaty, dishevelled man in half a bear's costume with a furry head in his lap. To make matters worse the bear-man was smoking. 'Look!' screamed Charlie. 'Smokey without his head on! Look, Nicolai! Look! It's a man!'

They stared at the grey-haired figure. He turned away. The boys

were half excited and half upset. His colleague appeared. 'Look!'
Charlie told her. 'It's a man!'

'Move on now, honey!' she barked.

'But look – Smokey doesn't have his head on!'

'Please move on, honey. Move on!'

I gathered the kids up and we returned to our seats. 'Is he called Smokey because he smokes?' asked Charlie.

From Grand Canyon station, we strolled to the rim. When I looked over I was mesmerised. Awesome is a word young Americans use excessively. Ask them about almost anything enjoyable and they'll tell you it was awesome. How was your vacation? Awesome. How was the football game? Awesome. How was your date? Dinner? Movie? Awesome. Awesome. Awesome... The word's original meaning has faded.

But stare into the Canyon and it bursts back to life. The sight is one of wonder – *truly awesome*.

Canyon means chasm and the Grand Canyon is the ultimate rocky abyss. Two hundred and seventy-seven miles long, between four and eighteen miles wide and over a mile deep, with the Colorado River flowing across its floor, it's a giant hole in the ground. The greatest man-made structures, in comparison, look like matchsticks.

Until six million years ago it was a hill. Then, for reasons still uncertain, the Colorado River crashed through it, the limestone and sandstone yielding quickly. Stare at the Canyon's intricately carved patterns and the wondrous, shimmering colours – reds, browns and whites of infinite hues – and it's easy to believe the myth that the Grand Canyon was once a Native American Garden of Eden.

I spotted some microscopic figures way below. You can hike down and up it on foot or mule (and spend a night at Phantom Lodge on the bottom). But some tours are so popular they have a year-long waiting list.

Up on the rim parents clung anxiously to their children. (Each year ten people take the fatal, so-called 'twelve-second tour'.) Nicolai tried climbing the low wall around the edge. I immediately yanked him down.

I held the boys while America took our pictures. But I didn't hold their hats. Nicolai yelled – the wind had caught his stetson. I put on his Virgin cap. He screamed again. That had also taken the 'twelve-second tour' (Today, his most vivid memory of our American trip is losing those beloved hats in the Grand Canyon.)

For the first time since Florida I heard numerous languages being spoken. Three million tourists visit the canyon each year. Until the 1920s the average stay was two to three weeks. Today it's two to three hours. But its magnificence is not diminished by the large human presence. The Grand Canyon is a symbol of America's scale. Nothing in Europe compares with its size or drama.

We entered a Hopi house – a 'historic landmark'. It was actually a store, selling 'Native American Arts and Crafts'. Soft Indian flute music wafted through speakers.

'Arrows!' exclaimed Charlie. (They were a hundred and ninety-nine dollars.)

'Yes and look – Indians put them in a quiver.'

'Why? To keep them warm?'

Another beautiful object was a multi-coloured, feathered man's bustle. 'Plains Indians used them in "fancy dresses" at powows,' said a label. 'This two-piece bustle is worn on the back just below the waist as part of the festive costume.' (It was eight hundred and forty-five dollars.)

In a glass case was a miniature papoose. 'A baby in a slipper,' said Nicolai. We bought Khelga a hand-painted tile.

Back on the train, loud-mouthed cowboys swaggered along the aisles. They looked a mean bunch. One, a whiskery fella, with a gun in his hand and a piercing, hyena's laugh, stopped in his tracks and stared at Charlie. 'How yah doin', pardner?' he growled. His voice was gravel-filled and menacing. Charlie froze – petrified. 'I said, "How yah doin?" You OK?'

'Actually,' I informed him. 'He's terrified of you.'

The figure leant down, moved close to Charlie and inhaled. But instead of uttering sweet reassurances he eyeballed my four-year-old, curled up a mean lip and snarled: 'So what you got to be terrified of, *bud*?' Charlie quivered. The cowboy strutted off.

Twenty minutes later, we screeched to a halt. Train staff shuffled. Two passengers winked at me. Expectant tension filled the air. Outside, mounted cowboys galloped past. Then they were aboard, storming the aisles. Shots rang out. In true saloon-bar style, Charlie and Nicolai dived under our table for cover. Charlie even covered his eyes.

A sheriff appeared. 'Where d'they go?' he hollered.

'Back there!' shouted passengers. The sheriff pursued them, reappearing later in triumph with all the crooks safely handcuffed.

'You can come out now, boys,' I said. Both re-emerged. They were silent all the way to Williams.

On the campground bus was an English family – Steve and Jane

162

Richardson with kids Chris, Sam and Adam. Steve was a British Army major halfway through a two-year exchange in Georgia. They had their own motorhome. We had a drink and next morning returned with them for the giant-screen Grand Canyon IMAX film. I left my RV in the campground, first moving it from the site into the owner's yard. Steve reversed me in, noticing the left brake-light and indicator didn't work. 'Two violations. I'd get them fixed if I were you...'

It was strange being a passenger in another RV. I sat in the back with the children. Like most American owners the Richardsons had an on-board VCR. Sam wore a brace on her teeth. 'I'm glad it's being done here,' said Jane. 'Most of her friends have them so she doesn't stand out.'

Why are Americans obsessed with orthodontics? I've got a friend with beautiful teeth. Within six months of marrying a (wonderful) American, she was wearing a brace (at the age of twenty-three).

All the children except Nicolai loved the film. As well as explorers it featured Grand Canyon wildlife (rabbits, mountain lions, scorpions, snakes...) Nicolai was terrified when a tarantula appeared – a hundred feet-long on the giant screen. (That night he had a nightmare. 'I don't like big spiders!' he sobbed.)

Back at the campground we said farewell to the Richardsons then drove to a RV service centre.

'Do you get many Europeans here?' I asked the mechanic as he checked some contact breakers.

'Sure – Germans, British, French. Actually, we don't get so many of *them*. But do you know? They piss us off so much, we charge them extra just for being French...

'So where are you *British* guys heading?' he asked us brightly.

'Los Angeles,' I said. 'But Sedona first of all.'

'Well, you take care, buddy. Sedona's real pretty but it's full o' weirdos...'

39 Sedona

The mechanic was right. Ever since a three-thousand-year-old Druid (called Albion) appeared to a travelling psychic in 1983 and told her there were seven vortices in the area (points at which, it is claimed, psychic energies can be channelled for personal and planetary harmony), Sedona has been a magnet for New Age practitioners ('Crystal Huggers', 'Moon Puppies' or 'Vortex Bunnies' as some of the locals label them).

But I'd booked a treat there – a night in a spa hotel. Arizona is famous for spa hotels (with treatments ranging from mud baths, to mind-and-body management) but most are further south and as we now lacked time I'd chosen Sedona.

Summer is low-season so it's a cheap time to try them. Temperatures can reach the hundreds but at least the heat's dry. Hotels attract visitors from nearby humid areas.

After visiting a local supermarket (where the lights mysteriously went out, plunging us temporarily into darkness – was this the effect of the vortex forces?) we reached 'Enchantment Resort'.

We were greeted at the gate by security man, Woody Conkle. 'Employee of the Month, April 1997'. He radioed the bellman. I parked the RV (in the tradesmen's yard) and we were taken to our room by electric car.

The kids opened a cupboard and found the mini-bar. Then they opened another and found the telly. Then they found a drum by the bed. The bathroom had cupboards big enough to hide in. And as I tipped the bellman I heard muffled giggles and a deep, thumping sound.

Seconds after arriving at the pool a woman demanded to know the children's birth dates. 'Aries and Libra – I can see that!' she bragged.

I got chatting with an Australian who later told his wife about our trip. 'Well, you're not getting *me* in a motorhome,' I overheard her say. 'It's all right for the man but what about the wife? Stuck in the flaming thing, cooking and cleaning all day... It's not much of a holiday for *her*. No, thank *you* very much...'

But I loved it. Summer motorhome-living was much easier than normal life in England. And both boys were happy so I was happy too.

I'd intended to have only a brief swim but the Sedona red-rock setting was soothingly seductive. Before New Age interest these rocks provided backdrops for Westerns. Today they are centres of pilgrimage – for healers, psychics, astrologists, ufologists (students of UFOs) and countless 'enlightened' tourists. We relaxed. The water was warm and the children were calm. Two hours imperceptibly slipped by. When we finally left, their backs were redder than the mystical rocks. I was furious with myself. For nine weeks I'd smeared them in factor fifty. But having run out, here in Arizona, I'd let them swim in factor six. I felt idiotic – like those Brits who go to the Costas, spend their entire first day on the beach and then in the evening, barely able to walk, say, sounding genuinely surprised: 'Isn't the Spanish sun strong?'

At that very moment I felt like saying: 'Isn't the Arizona sun strong?'

Back in the room I splattered them in Aloe Vera. Luckily, they weren't burnt. (They'd had nine weeks adapting). But I did feel a fool for needing the warning.

Enchantment was enchanting but I couldn't enjoy it properly. A massage would have been nice but at seventy dollars for fifty minutes I gave it a miss. Childcare was also expensive. In fact my budget was so limited we couldn't even afford the restaurant. So, like a Special Air Service commando on a mission, I slipped away to the RV and, under cover of darkness, sneaked food supplies to our room – bananas, apples, oranges, bread, tomatoes, ham, cornflakes and milk. The next day all evidence was removed. Not by the cleaners though. Definitely not! I couldn't have them espying my illicit rubbish. I carefully put the garbage into (specially brought in) bin-liners then, when the bellman collected us, he gently placed them on his electric car as if they were the finest Gucci cases. He drove us to the RV and, with tip-inspiring respect, dutifully unloaded all our crap. He even placed the bin-bags in our motorhome. One stank! Five dollars killed his curiosity. But I did feel rather shoddy. A nasty little cheapskate British tourist.

I felt even more cheapskate when I asked America to lend me twenty dollars. I'd borrowed off Julia when I'd run out of cash before but had really hated doing so. 'Don't worry,' she'd said. 'I don't need efficiency at the moment. That's what it'll be like in my permanent German job. It's nice to enjoy some British chaos now...'

We'd clocked up extra miles but Sedona had been fun. Clean sheets had been joyful and the scenery gorgeous. 'I loved the red rocks,' said Charlie.

After stopping off downtown (overrun by New Age emporia) we visited Slide Rock Park. This takes its name from a natural red rock slide in a creek. The park was packed. We queued for the slide, but standing in the water proved difficult (the rocks were slippery and the creek flowed fast). We awaited our turn and having finally reached it I put a child on each knee and launched into the freezing, fast-flowing water. The two boys screamed. They must have felt like we were riding the rapids of the Grand Canyon. At the bottom both were wet and furious. 'Stupid man!' bawled Nicolai. 'I hate that slide! Stupid, stupid man! You knew we hated that slide!'

Back on the road the highway was full of empty school buses. The autumn term was about to start.

40 Wild Kids

'Eleven weeks with your kids while your wife stays at home?' a camper had said to me back east. 'That must have taken some organising, sir. Did you plan every stage of your trip?' (I didn't plan my kids so I could hardly plan this adventure.)

'Not really,' I replied. 'I take each stage as it comes.'

I'd booked the RV in May, we'd left in June and collected the air tickets from Trailfinders in London the day before. Organisation isn't my strong point, which is how I had messed up our hotel reservation.

Sedona is south-east of the Grand Canyon and we were travelling west. That had meant a rather pointless backtrack.

We meandered our way back to I-40 West and checked into a campground where we were given a space on what felt like a low-life estate. Around us teenagers horse-played, shouted, snogged and smoked. Adults sat passively, knocking back cans. Kids in the playground looked wild. The wildest was no more than five. His parents were invisible and he was uncontrollable. He booted swings, ran up the slide backwards and scrapped with children twice his age and size. After telling two parents (who had the audacity to reprimand him – albeit timidly) to 'go suck', he span around some eight-year-olds so fast on the roundabout they pleaded, squealing, to get off. Satisfied with the chaos caused by his reign of terror he vaulted over the playground fence and left.

Charlie and Nicolai were, thankfully, well away from him, playing with some Tonka toys lent by the owner's father. I don't know where the son was, but dad was getting inebriated fast. 'Heh, man – you from England? You want a beer?' He passed me a Bud from his cooler. 'I went to England once with the Air Force. They flew me from Las Vegas to Brentwood – for two days only. Didn't see much of England but I remember getting *pissed in a pub* ...' He repeated the phrase with relish, savouring the p-sounds as he pushed them off his lips. '*Ye–p! P–issed in a p–ub* ...! We had a lot of fun that night in

England. Then they flew me back to Vegas. Haven't been there since. Heh man, you want another beer?'

He told me he was a construction worker from Lake Havasu City on the Colorado River. 'It's where London Bridge is – they shipped it over and rebuilt it. You ever been on London Bridge? You should go there, man, if you're from England. I'm enjoyin' a break from the heat. I been building an elementary school these last two months. Laying slabs in a hundred and twenty degrees heat. The weather here is air-conditioning for me, man. Yep, this wind is beautiful. Heh, you want another beer?'

I left him to his memories and his cooler. We had little food so we dined on the campground. Steak with trimmings for only eight dollars sounded a pretty good deal.

Monique and Herbie were the catering team. Poor old Herbie looked like he should have hung up his spatula years ago. Dressed in shorts out of which protruded his bony, bald legs, he had problems hearing and stuttered.

'Which one is well done?' I asked.

'W–w–what d'yah mean, well done?' said Herbie. 'I thought you wanted f–f–four mediums...' I took it anyway. All the steaks were excellent.

That night America met a Spaniard. 'He's from the Basque country so I'm going to buy some beer. Don't bother waiting up for me.'

I didn't expect her back until late. But she returned – very respectably – at ten-thirty p.m. She went to bed and left me reading.

Both boys slept soundly but I tossed and turned. This was my first night in my new sleeping bag. I was wishing I'd bought a better one. It made my skin itch and let in cold air. What could I have expected for only fourteen dollars?

41 Route 66

You might be wondering how I've managed to get this far without mentioning Route 66.

The 'Mother Road' (or 'Main Street of America' to give it just two of its many names) has progressed from ancient Indian trails to a modern super highway. Until 1984 (and completion of the Interstate system) it remained the main link between Chicago and Los Angeles.

Its modern history began in 1857 after the discovery of gold in California provoked a surge of emigration west. Edward Beale, a former US Navy lieutenant who had trekked across the continent as a scout and messenger, was commissioned to build a safe, all-weather wagon road from north-east Arizona to the mouth of California's Mojave River.

Beale surveyed the road across the thirty-fifth Parallel following Indian trails.

When the Atlantic and Pacific Railroad (later to become the Santa Fé Railway) began construction of a line which would span the United States, the thirty-fifth Parallel was the chosen route again. The track often paralleled Beale's path.

In 1914 the National Old Trails Highway, the predecessor of Route 66, was completed. And by 1916, a bridge across the Colorado River had opened.

When Route 66 was officially named in 1926, only about eight hundred of its two thousand two hundred miles were paved.

Surfacing was completed in the 1930s and during the great depression it was the way west for thousands fleeing the drought-torn Great Plains states (like the farmers in John Steinbeck's *The Grapes Of Wrath*).

World War II brought massive troop movements. And after the war, many servicemen relocated west. The US Highway Association was formed in 1947 with the aim of improving roads and stimulating tourism. And the National Highway Interstate System was instigated in the 1950s.

Communities and businesses along Route 66 feared that I-40 would end their way of life. In many cases it did. Some towns were bypassed and tourist income ended (while others on the new route experienced a business boom).

But in the last twenty years Historic Route 66 Associations have grown up along stretches of the old road. Some travellers follow it deliberately. Surface quality varies widely (so it's not the best sole option for a motorhome).

But in this part of Arizona it's generally well-preserved. 'Historic Route 66' markers indicate the old road. Some of the restored buildings (museums, visitors' centers and diners) make an interesting stop-off and original motels make a good alternative to the usual, characterless chains.

By this point I'd exceeded my mileage allowance and still had another thousand to go. But I didn't care. I turned up the radio and got into Route 66 mood. A classic rock station played songs from my teenage years – Santana, Roxy Music, David Bowie, Iggy Pop... 'Hi, I'm John,' said the DJ, 'and 1970s music is my bag...'

There was a wide choice of stations near Flagstaff – smooth rock, hard rock, soft rock, heavy rock... That was just as well because John and his classic rock faded pretty soon. Then, as all the others faded too, it was time for America to dig up more cassettes. Oasis soon filled the air.

Between Flagstaff and Seligman we cruised on and off Route 66. (Parts of it have been covered by I-40 while in other areas the old road runs parallel to the Interstate.) At Seligman we stopped for shakes at Delgadillo's Snow Cap Drive-In (an original 1950s roadside diner). Then it was Route 66 all the way to Kingman, pausing only at Peach Springs to talk to a motorcyclist who was raving about a race with a Santa Fé railroad engine. 'It was so neat, man. The driver was smiling and sounding his horn and I had the wind in my hair as I flew past...'

We arrived at the Kingman campground as the sun began to set. The sky was a mix of pink, yellow and orange pastel shades.

An elderly man driving an electric cart led us to our campground space. As I killed my engine Nicolai started screaming. He was angry with America. I don't know what she'd done (probably refused to massage his forehead). But he got furiously, embarrassingly, upset. 'I *hate* America! America is horrible! I think America is stupid!'

The old man surveyed me suspiciously (he probably thought we were about to burn the flag). 'It's quite all right,' I said, reassuring him.

'I *hate* America!' repeated Nicolai.

The man scrutinised me. 'Heh,' I said, 'he's not talking about the country. I *promise*! Our au pair girl's Spanish and *her* name is America... Honestly! Her name *is* America. They've had an argument. He's not talking about the country...'

The man looked unconvinced. Nicolai restarted. 'I *really* hate America! I do!'

'Nicolai,' I shouted. '*Be quiet now!* America – come and tell us your name.'

'America,' she said. 'America Sanchez.'

'America Sanchez..?' said the old boy, relaxing. 'Your name is really America?'

'Yes,' said our au pair, obligingly.

'Well, that is a bea–ooou–tiful name...'

42 Further Embarrassment in Kingman

My debt to America outstanding, a convenient bank was next morning's aim. I pulled into a parking-lot. A local had informed me that Smith's Food and Drug contained a branch of Wells Fargo Bank.

He was right. I sighed in relief. This had been easy. No messing with parking downtown. I awaited my turn and when I reached the cashier, took out my trusty Barclaycard. 'Two hundred dollars cash, please,' I said.

'No problem,' replied the smiling woman.

I smiled back. She swiped my card. I waited patiently. She swiped again and then whispered something through the glass.

'Sorry...?' I quizzed, not catching her words.

She whispered again. I still couldn't hear. 'I beg your pardon.'

She carried on whispering. 'I'm afraid I really can't hear...'

'*Your card's been declined!*' she blurted out loud.

'Oh...' I mumbled, calmly. 'That's strange...'

I pulled another credit card out of my wallet. She examined it closely. 'Expired!' she announced.

'Expired?' I took the card.

'Expired...' she repeated, irritated.

Thankfully I had still one more credit card up my sleeve. Good old MBNA. They're an American bank and have been marketing aggressively in Britain. Knowing that extra cards would be useful in the States I'd applied for one and received it only days before our trip.

'Okay,' she sighed, wearily, 'let's try this...'

'We're in luck,' she sneered. 'Two hundred dollars...' She counted out the greenbacks without asking which particular notes I wanted. I retreated, relieved, to the RV.

When I recounted the embarrassing incident, Charlie's response was: 'Did the bank have stuffed animals on its walls?'

'No. It didn't, Charlie...' Even in Arizona, *supermarket* banks don't have stuffed animals on their walls.

At Lake Mead (thirty miles from Vegas and one of America's largest man-made lakes – a result of the Hoover Dam) we stopped to admire the gorgeous view – mountains, canyons and ravines surround the water (nicknamed 'the jewel of the desert'). This is a popular spot but visitors savour it for an average of only ninety seconds. America timed the cars. They would stop, drivers and passengers would get out, glance around, take a photo, get back in their car and drive away. We probably qualified for the world record Lake Mead stop. We pulled up, looked at the view, walked around the RV, got back in the RV, cooked lunch, walked around again, stared at the view, had a drink, and eventually drove off – total time: fifty-two minutes.

It was interesting to car and people spot. Half the vehicles had Californian plates. Plenty were snazzy models – like the occupants. Men were better dressed than most we'd seen before. Girls were often sexy and glamorous. Couples would pose for photos and kiss. Several asked me to take their pictures.

Further west we stopped at the Hoover Dam, the highest concrete dam in the western hemisphere. The seven hundred and twenty-seven feet tall dam (made from nearly four and a half million cubic yards of concrete – enough to build a two-lane highway from the West Coast to New York) blocks the Colorado River and supplies hydro-electric power to half a million homes.

Dusk was falling fast. 'Daddy,' said Charlie, 'can we have a quick swim in the lake?'

'That's not a lake, Charles. That's the Hoover Dam – the biggest dam in the western hemisphere...'

'Yes, but can we please have a swim in it?'

43 Arrival in Vegas

We arrived in Vegas as darkness fell and drove to the KOA. The registration office was thronging with Brits and Germans. It made me feel glad that we'd visited places most Europeans hadn't reached. The man booking me in was called Norm. 'I think we can find a space — especially for a British gentleman...'

'Thanks very much.'

'You bet. My wife's from London...'

'Yeh? Whereabouts?'

'Fulham...'

'That's where my nursery is!' exclaimed Charlie, excitedly.

'Really, young man? And where exactly in Fulham is your nursery?'

'Moore Park Road,' I said.

'Know it well,' declared Norm. 'Near Safeway — beyond the Broadway. My wife grew up there... She lived near the Normand Arms pub.'

'That's near where *we* live — except we're in West Kensington...'

'Now what was her road called...?'

Norm picked the phone up and summoned his wife. 'Eileen — I've got someone from London who'd like to meet you.' Seconds later she appeared. 'Now, honey, would you tell this gentleman where you are from.'

'Well, first I was in Delaford Street and then in Halford Road — just off the North End Road.'

'That's right near us,' I said.

'Small world,' said Norm. 'Crazy, huh?'

'I lived there years ago,' mused Eileen. 'Our area was pretty derelict after the war... Normand Park was a bomb site then. And Lillie Road was battered... Oh yes, it took a hammering in the war...'

Once we were registered Norm handed me a bag of promotional goodies. Charlie wrenched it from my hand. 'What's this?' he asked, spotting an ad for a 'Sexy Magic' show.

America studied the *What's On* magazine. 'Spice Girls!' said Charlie, pointing to a picture. But they weren't the real Spice Girls – just part of a wannabes show. A blonde camper in a Union Jack swimming costume, strutted by. 'Look, another Spice Girl!' said Charlie.

We had steak for dinner – a couple of T-bones and two Porterhouses, carved up and shared between the four of us. 'Aren't they delicious?' I said to America. 'Isn't this steak wonderful, boys?'

'You could convert a vegetarian,' said America. But meat in the States is excellent. (And cheap.)

The Las Vegas meal was complimented by Sam Adams beer, a brew from a Boston micro-brewery. I'd moved on from Budweiser. And Schlitz. And Michelob... The big names were tasteless compared to this.

Early next morning the sun pierced the RV. Despite my attempts to block out the light – with sleeping bags, towels, and T-shirts against the windows – the kids were running around at six a.m. We went to the office for some postcards. Ursula and Dave were at the front desk.

'Mr Dave, sir,' said a dishevelled woman. 'If I took a pack of cigarettes, could I bring you the cash later?'

'I'm sorry, honey,' said Mr Dave. 'You know we're not allowed to do that...'

The woman was a permanent resident. There were plenty on this KOA, including our neighbours, Stanley and Wendy. They'd lived on the campground for years.

'Do you like it here?' I asked.

'It's OK,' said Wendy. 'Except when the heat gets out of control and the sewer ventilation pipe stinks...'

I asked them if they visited casinos. 'We sure do – usually twice a day...'

Before driving downtown we posted our cards in the campground office post box. One end of the store contained poker, fruit, video and pinball machines. While I bought some juice the kids pressed some buttons. 'Would you take those kids away from those machines,' demanded Dave, aggressively.

'But they're not gambling,' I replied in a tone he obviouly interpreted as insolence.

175

'Listen!' he exclaimed, with fury. 'I don't want a five-hundred-dollar fine – *and I'm sure you don't either, sir!* Because Nevada state law strictly prohibits children from going anywhere near those machines...'

'Then why have them openly displayed in your shop, next to the children's games?' But I only thought those words. 'Yes, of course,' I said, obligingly. 'Charlie, Nicolai – come here now...'

Keeping the children away from slots was a problem. Only minutes later, after filling up with gas, the boys and I went to pay my bill. In the station shop were noisy, hypnotic, flashing machines which instantly magnetised the kids. 'Sir,' said the cashier, 'would you take your children away from those now. Nevada State Law prohibits children from going near machines...'

It was worse downtown. Many casinos are in hotels with family entertainments. Frequently we would be obliged to cross a sea of buzzing, ringing, flashing slot machines, to find something of interest to us all – like the restaurant or an entertainment area. As we waded through, the children would investigate. Immediately a voice boomed out: 'Sir, will you take your children away from those machines. Nevada State Law prohibits children from loitering near them...'

I explained to Charlie and Nicolai that these fascinating objects were for gambling. 'What's gambling?' asked Charlie.

'It's when you spend money to try to win more money. For example, if you put money in this machine, press the button, and get three fruits the same, you could win one hundred dollars.'

'Can we have a go?'

'*I'll* have a try...'

I put in fifty cents, pushed a button and the machine gamely spat out six quarters. 'That's good,' said Charlie. 'Did you win a hundred dollars?'

'Seventy five cents. But gamblers don't usually win anything...'

'I want to gamble when I'm a man.'

One way Vegas hotels entice you into their casinos is by providing extremely cheap food. At the Luxor Hotel we had a buffet lunch, as much as we could possibly eat and drink, for only five dollars ninety-nine.

The kids could barely understand the concept. 'Can I really have a thousand Cokes?' Nicolai asked, twinkling in wonder.

We certainly got our money's worth. I ate until my stomach wept. America was modest, except with the fruit. The boys consumed vast quantities of sausages and ice-cream. To show his appreciation at the end of the meal Nicolai paid an ancient compliment. He farted. Extremely loudly. I stared disapprovingly. 'Oops,' he said sweetly, 'my bottom coughed.' Charlie passed wind at even higher volume. (Then, to my embarrassment, so did I — we were like the cowboys in the baked beans scene from Mel Brookes's *Blazing Saddles*. America remained silent and dignified.)

'Let's ignore this,' I suggested as the boys tittered. Then Charlie let rip a real humdinger. He giggled, spluttered and wept with delight until he composed himself to recite a short ditty. 'Pardon me for being rude. It was not me — it was my food...' More uncontrollable mirth.

I didn't know my boy knew such a rhyme. 'Who taught you that?' I asked, shocked.

'Jim...'

Jim is one of my brothers. I'm the oldest of four boys and he is the next one down. Uncle Jim has been corrupting small Collins boys since, at the age of ten, he accompanied our brother Dan, then five, to school. He'd divert to the park and test Dan's reading skills by showing him smutty graffiti on swings.

'Has Jim taught you other rhymes?' I asked.

'Yup!'

'What?'

'Yum, yum, pig's tum, stick it up your mother's b...'

'*Enough!*'

The boys exploded into titters again. I paid and we left the restaurant.

44 Family Entertainment in Sin City

'No, this is not a good town for psychedelic drugs. Reality itself is too twisted.' So wrote Hunter S. Thompson in *Fear and Loathing in Las Vegas*. I've never taken psychedelic drugs but it didn't take long to see what he meant.

Ironically, Nevada was the first US state to outlaw gambling. It became legalized in 1931 (supposedly to raise taxes for schools) but, for fifteen years, Las Vegas remained a sleepy desert town.

It took a gangster, Bugsy Siegel, to see the potential of it all. In 1946 he opened The Flamingo, a plush, pink neon-lit, hotel/casino, on what's now known as The Strip.

The Flamingo set the style for other hotel/casinos and established the city's links with organised crime. It also established the lure (still active today) of enticing gamblers with bargain-priced rooms and food.

Las Vegas, basically, divides into two parts – the Strip and downtown (known as Glitter Gulch). Downtown casinos are said to offer better odds but the most extravagant hotels are on the Strip.

During the 1990s, Las Vegas has attempted to enter the family market. Massive investments have been made in mind-blowingly gaudy places like Excalibur, The Luxor and MGM Grand. They still have casinos but are really self-contained, themed, fantasy-lands.

The Luxor is a thirty-storey bronze and glass pyramid, themed (unsurprisingly) on Ancient Egypt. A Sphinx guards the entrance and inside there's a replica of Tutankhamun's tomb. The most powerful artificial light beam ever created shines up form the pyramid's apex (paying tribute to the belief that a dead Pharaoh's soul rose directly towards the skies). It's visible from planes circling Los Angeles, two hundred and fifty miles west.

From Ancient Egypt we strolled to the Middle Ages – Excalibur is a castle full of jousters and jesters (where guests are paged as 'Lady' or 'Lord'). Then it was Treasure Island with its own flaming galleons, on to Mirage with its erupting volcanos and into Circus Circus for acrobats, tightrope walkers, and fire-eaters.

The kids adored Vegas but our problem was the heat. Walking outside had us sweating in seconds. After a peek in Caesar's Palace (venue for big boxing contests – and full of strutting Roman centurions) we made our way to the RV.

I'd left it in the MGM Grand lot but finding our way out of the hotel proved difficult. The walk involved a trans-casino trek. *En route* I stuck two quarters in a slot. A shower of coins rained down. I scooped out the money and counted three dollars. 'You're great at gambling,' said Charlie.

In the lobby, Popeye and Olive Oyl were on walkabout. We grabbed a quick photo and raced to the parking-lot. There I fed the boys banana sandwiches.

By the time we were sailing down Las Vegas Boulevard they were asleep in the back. But leaving the freeway proved difficult. The traffic was furious and exit roads appeared (often randomly) on either side. To make matters worse my wing mirrors were loose. When signs for my exit appeared on the left I positioned myself in a lane on that side. Seconds later I flew past the exit on the right.

I pulled in at a gas station and studied my map. Back on the freeway my mirrors flapped wildly. I bawled at America for help. She rushed to the front, wound down the window and gamely stuck out her head, gesticulating to cars that we were about to change lanes. But each time she screamed 'Go! Now! Go!', vehicles behind us sped up. America thrashed her arms round. But drivers accelerated, desperate to keep our motorhome out. Rush hour in Nashville had been challenging but Las Vegas drivers were the meanest so far.

We arrived at the campground at eight-thirty p.m. The boys were still sleeping so I put them to bed. Both then awoke, complaining about the heat. I cleaned their teeth, placed an ice-cube wrapped in kitchen paper on their eyes and gently placed them back in their beds.

America was weary but I felt the call of the casino. Boulder Street Station, a local haunt, was only a stroll away. By the time she was lying next to Nicolai I was leaving. 'I'll be less than an hour,' I said. And shot off into the warm, balmy night.

45 Beginner's Luck

Just before the swimming pool a black cat crossed my path. At the campground gate three security men stood chatting. 'Is it safe to walk to Boulder Street Station?' I asked, feeling like the innocent boy in town.

'Sure,' said a guard. 'You're on the main drag. Five minutes walk. It's not a problem...'

'Thanks,' I said. And strolled around the corner before I started running. Adrenaline ran through me. This was the first night that I'd left America with the kids in the RV. I felt a small, illicit thrill. But fears coursed through my mind. What if one was sick? What if some nutter knocked at the door? But I had to do this. I couldn't come to Vegas and not have a flutter. I would go in, buy a hundred dollars worth of chips, stick them on one odds-on roulette bet. And leave. Come what may, I would be back in 20 minutes.

My adrenaline buzz increased as I saw a neon sign: 'Topless Girls – Fabulous Freemont – The Girls From Glitter Gulch.' My knees trembled. My heart palpitated. I sprinted towards the casino. Then I paused for breath at a bus stop shelter. On it was a poster promoting St Jude.

St Jude – Patron Saint of Hopeless Causes

St Jude will pray for you
Ask him for help every day
Your request will be granted
Have faith
It works

I didn't need St Jude. Not yet anyway. So I ran on ahead, stopped for a deep breath... And dived into the massive casino. Boulder Street Station was a wonder. It had been one thing crossing hotel casinos with the children. But now, alone at night, with money to burn... I felt like a virgin in a brothel. Acres of floor space were covered with

180

machines. Entranced, hardened gamblers fed slots robotically. All looked in need of St Jude.

But where were the roulette tables? Spying them at the far end I swept past a sea of slot machines. Reaching the destination I instantly lost my nerve. One hundred dollars on a single bet? This was madness. I needed to ease myself into the gambling mood.

'A dollar's worth of nickels, please,' I said to a change-trolley girl.

'A dollar?' I felt ashamed at the small amount.

But armed with the coins I chose my machine. It was a bad choice. Had I been smart I would have looked for one that had been fed by some luckless punter. But I obviously chose one that had just paid out a jackpot. It paid me a couple of ten cents wins but my dollar's worth of nickels disappeared fast.

I circled what I thought was a roulette table and tried to get the feel of a game. It turned out to be a crap table and I ended up hemmed-in behind it with the dealer. 'Looking for a job?' asked a voice from above. It was the supervisor, sitting in a high-chair.

'Sorry, I didn't realise... How do you play this?'

'The dealer will help you.' But there were already a dozen hardened gamblers at the table. I couldn't ask about the rules.

I didn't want to play crap anyway. Nor twenty-one. Nor baccarat. Nor poker. I wanted to play roulette. But finding a table that wasn't crowded was difficult. I circled a few to find one that felt good. I didn't mind waiting but it had to feel right.

But no particular table felt right so I found another change girl and bought some more nickels.

Some machines displayed a notice above them which said temptingly: 'Get Carded – Get Food'. I was hungry so I decided to get carded. I filled in a form and a promotions assistant handed me my Boulder Street card. 'So can I get free food now?' I asked.

'Well, you get points for every time you play,' she said. 'Your card records them and when you've got enough you get the food.'

'So how many points do I get for playing?'

'Well, some slots get you one point and others give you two.'

'And how many points do I need to get food?'

She produced a redemption menu. 'Well, to get a pretzel – you need twelve hundred and fifty. For a small yoghurt – seven hundred...' I wished I hadn't bothered. Spending hundreds of dollars for a pretzel seemed ridiculous.

Back at the crap table I saw the supervisor. 'Where do I get chips please?'

'Any table you want. The dealer will exchange them for cash...'

I chose a roulette table and ordered a drink. I knew booze was free but was unable to master even this system. 'Could I have a Piña Colada, please?' I asked a six-feet-something waitress. She was wearing flat shoes, a micro miniskirt and tights that disappeared visibly up her backside. 'Not my patch honey,' she replied in a rasping voice. 'But I'll tell the girl who covers here...'

'Forget the drinks,' I thought. 'I'm going to do what I came in for...'

An elderly Hispanic woman with two whisky tumblers and a pile of chips stacked up in front of her, moved along to make space for me. I squeezed myself in and displayed my ready cash. The dealer knew a rookie when he saw one. He motioned with his rake as though I was deaf, inviting me to put down my money. I counted out one hundred dollars. He raked in the notes and pushed out some counters – forty, in various colours.

'Place your bets now,' he said. The Hispanic woman placed a dozen. Other players followed. I decided to hang loose for this one.

The dealer span the ball. It landed on 29. The dealer raked in the losing chips.

As soon as he had paid out I placed my bet. The 1-18 square was directly in front of me. I piled all my chips on it and watched the ball spin. Then I shut my eyes, prayed, crossed my fingers and sent every positive vibe I could muster up to that little, spinning silver ball. Then I heard it clink into place. I opened my eyes to see it nestled neatly in 12. My face cracked with joy. I beamed imbecilically. I'd never been a poker-face. The losing chips were raked in. My pile was doubled. I had a hundred dollars instant profit.

I was momentarily tempted to try my luck again – by betting on 18-36. But I resisted. And when the ball slid into 17 I felt relieved I hadn't pushed things. I cashed in the chips but just before I left, managed to get a Piña Colada (complete with cherry on a stick and paper umbrella – hardly a pro gambler's tipple) out of a husky waitress with tiny lizard eyes and a huge, heaving bosom. I gave her a five dollar tip. 'Why, thank you sweetheart,' she said.

Walking along the neon-lit highway I picked up from a news-rack what I assumed was a listings magazine. Flicking through the pages I was the innocent boy in town again. Under misty shots of pornographically posed girls, were temptingly over-the-top claims: 'Ex Cheerleader working my way through college.' Or: 'I'm the bitch your mother warned you about.' Or: 'The hottest girl in town. Try me now...'

Men were featured too – Wayne, Jason, Brad and two Brians among them. All greased and tanned like Chippendales and 'available in minutes in your hotel room'.

I binned the mag and ran back to my children.

'America,' I whispered, half trying to wake her. I wanted to give her my news. 'Guess what...? I won a hundred dollars...'

But America only snored. So I went to bed.

46 Invitation to a Wedding

The priority next morning was to get the mirrors fixed. I drove to the local Cruise America depot where a technician screwed them down. 'Yeh, we've had problems with this Ford design. I've seen mirrors held in place with tape, glue, tacks or anything. But it's not a problem on the Chevy. There you go bud. All taken care of... Have a great trip.' I got back in the RV and drove downtown.

The other major casino area is downtown around Fremont Street. Parking here proved a problem. Every lot seemed to have a STRICTLY CARS ONLY notice or barriers saying CLEARANCE – 6' 6". Eventually I found one adjacent to a hotel with a PATRONS AND EMPLOYEES ONLY sign. Further ahead another said: GUESTS – SHOW YOUR KEY TO THE ATTENDANT.

But I couldn't see an attendant so I parked. As I manoeuvred I saw a security man on a bicycle (you see lots of cycling cops and security guards in Vegas). 'Excuse me,' I said. 'Is there an attendant here?'

'Nope,' he replied.

'So do I need to show a key?'

'Just stick it there. We get buses, campers and employees from other casinos parking in this lot. Don't you worry. They won't do nothing at all...'

We got out of the RV and walked towards Fremont Street. America carried a cup of iced water and was complaining, surprisingly, about the heat. 'But you're a Nicaraguan Spanish woman. You must be used to the heat...'

'Yes, but this is different. And I've always hated strong sun...'

At the junction with Las Vegas Boulevard we passed a raggedly dressed man sitting in a sprawl on the street. I walked hand in hand with the boys. 'Sir!' said the man. 'Sir, excuse me, please...'

'What?' I replied.

'Sir...' He looked at me, piteously. 'Sir – you are *such* a lucky man...'

'Thanks...'

'You're welcome, sir...' And with that he wept – uncontrollable, high-volume sobs.

We passed a casino with a woman at the door who thrust a wad of dollars in my hand. They were fake, of course – slot machine vouchers which I didn't want.

'Go on,' she said, 'come in and try. Nothing to lose. But you can't take the kids...'

'So where will they go?' I asked.

'Oh... Well take the coupons, anyway.'

'But I don't want them.'

'Well give them to your boys.'

'They'll throw them on the streets.'

'That doesn't matter. There you go...'

We carried on down Fremont. The boys saw a pink neon sign: 'The Girls From Glitter Gulch. Fabulous Fremont's Famous Topless Bar'.

'Who's that girl with the bendy legs?' asked Charlie. 'Is she a cowboy?' (She was wearing a cowboy hat.)

'Can we see the cowgirl?' asked Nicolai.

'We're not staying in Glitter Gulch,' I said.

Continuing down Las Vegas Boulevard we saw the 'Wee Kirk o' the Heather'. A sign proclaimed it the 'Oldest Wedding Chapel in Las Vegas'.

'Heh boys,' I said, 'let's take a photo. This is where people get married.'

America took our picture then Nicolai said he needed the loo.

'You'll have to wait,' I said. 'There are no toilets here.'

'But I need a wee now...'

I scooped him up and knocked on the 'Wee Kirk's' front door. A dead ringer for the New York comedian, Jackie Mason, answered. 'I'm really sorry to bother you,' I said. 'We're just passing and my little boy desperately needs the bathroom. Would it be possible to use your facilities?'

'No problem,' said the man. He was wearing shorts with knee-length socks. His hair looked very probably dyed. 'Come right in.' He led us through the chapel to the door of a pink bathroom. 'Go ahead. Please take your time...'

Nicolai did his business. I did as well. Then Charlie needed a wee too. While I washed my hands Nicolai grabbed the airspray and sprayed a fragrant haze around the room. We left the bathroom smelling of 'Nature's Way'.

'Thank you so much,' I said. 'That was very kind.'

'No problem,' said the man. 'Y'all from England?'

I said we were. And asked about marrying in Vegas.

The guy's name was Ken and he was a 'wedding co-ordinator'. 'Well it's easier to marry here than in many other states,' he said. 'For example, in California, you need to take a blood test and get all kinds of other bits and pieces ... Here, you just go to the courthouse and buy a marriage licence. Costs you seventy-five cents. However, people sometimes forget that just because it's easier to get married doesn't mean it's easier to get divorced here. You have to go to Mexico if you want a quick divorce.'

'And are Las Vegas marriages recognised around the world?'

'Sure,' said Ken. 'Why not take our pricelist?' And he handed me a leaflet outlining the 'Kirk's' charges (which started at thirty-nine dollars for the 'Basic "I Do" Package' — chapel, music, witness and souvenir scroll — rising to ninety-nine dollars for the 'Wedding to Remember Package' — photos, a video and 'use of silk flower bouquet'). As I scanned the list an elegant, mature couple entered.

'Can we get married today?' asked the woman bluntly.

'Sure,' said Ken. 'Do you have a licence from the courthouse?'

'Right here,' said the woman.

'Well, that's great ...'

'So what are your prices?'

Ken gave a summary of his packages. 'And can we pay by credit card?'

'Unfortunately, no,' said Ken. 'But there's an ATM right over there.' And he pointed beyond the building to the other side of Las Vegas Boulevard.

'Okay,' she said. 'We'll take the basic package.'

Ken took their details. They were Carmella and Thomas from Wayne in New Jersey. Thomas was seventy-one and divorced with three children (the oldest was fifty-one). Carmella was sixty-four and had never been married.

'What made you want to marry in Las Vegas?' I asked nosily.

'Well, we've been together for over twenty years,' said Carmella, 'and if we don't do this and something happens there could be problems — legal, financial, that kind of thing. We're gonna have a bigger ceremony later, but we felt if we told Tom's kids they'd want to arrange everything and then it might all get out of hand. This is an easy way of doing it. *And* we get a vacation too.' They had chosen the 'Wee Kirk' because it had looked 'friendly and not too expensive'.

'Okay,' said Ken. 'Please take a seat. The minister will be here very soon...'

Carmella and Tom sat down. Then I asked a cheeky question.

'Carmella...Tom...Tell me to get lost if I'm being forward. But we're from England... Would it would be possible to come to your wedding?'

'Of course,' said Carmella sweetly. 'We would both love that... Wouldn't we, Tom?' Tom hummed agreement and I skipped outside to invite America.

As we were waiting another couple entered. 'I'm sorry,' said Ken. 'These people had a four o' clock appointment. Carmella, Tom – would you mind being patient just until these good folks are done?'

'Go right ahead,' said Carmella. And then a third couple arrived.

'How much is a wedding?' said the man in a southern twang. He and his fiancée were from Arkansas. 'And *what* is a *kirk*? And what the *heck* is *heather*?'

Ken showed him the prices, explained that a 'kirk' was a small Scottish church and that 'heather' was a 'lucky Scottish flower'. The man decided on the thirty-nine-dollar 'Basic "I Do" Package', and he and his wife-to-be sat down too.

'Okay,' said Ken when the minister arrived. 'Carmella, Tom – we'll do our four o'clocks then it's you...' He glanced at the Arkansas couple. 'And then when they're through we'll do you...' The first two were out in nine minutes forty seconds (I timed them) and Ken called the next couple in.

'Carmella, Tom – please come this way. And, of course, all your British guests...'

'And Spanish...' added America.

I took off my panama and ordered the kids to remove their baseball caps.

'Why?' asked Nicolai.

'Just do it,' I said.

Ken led Carmella to the back of the tiny chapel. Tom stood opposite the minister in the front. We were two pews behind. A

Barbara Streisand love-song wafted through hidden speakers.

The minister summoned Carmella and Ken led her gallantly, arm in arm, to the front. When she reached Tom she gave him a loving look. I swallowed. The boys spluttered. And the minister gave a homily on the meaning of modern marriage emphasising the need to stop watching TV occasionally. 'Communication is sooohh important these days,' he said. 'So Carmella, Tom... Try and take time out to switch off that TV and talk together at least once a week...'

The couple made their vows and the minister pronounced them man and wife. 'You may kiss the bride, Thomas,' he said. Thomas kissed Carmella and, with a lump in my throat (I lie not – this was touching), I rushed to kiss Carmella too.

'Congratulations,' I said. And shook Tom's hand. 'And thank you so much for inviting us.'

'Thank you so much for coming,' said Carmella. 'We really appreciated it. And wasn't it a beautiful service?'

'It was,' I said, sincerely. I'd really felt moved.

Charlie and Nicolai kissed the bride. Nicolai ran to the bathroom and grabbed the airspray. Charlie snatched it and sprayed 'Nature's Way' round the chapel. America kissed the bride and groom. I asked for a photo in the garden. I took it and promised them a copy. Then it was time to leave Las Vegas.

'Thank you so much again for coming,' said Carmella. She was dewy-eyed. 'We were really so pleased you were there.'

'Yeh, thanks a lot,' added Tom.

'Good luck,' I said. And we headed back to our RV.

47 Arrival in Los Angeles

'Daddy,' said Charlie *en route* to the RV. 'Why was that old man marrying that old lady? Didn't they get married when they were young?'

'Well...' I said. 'Sometimes it takes a long time for a man to find the right wife. Or for a woman to find the right husband. And some people never marry. And other people marry when they're old...'

'You weren't old when you married mummy, were you? Did you marry mummy in Las Vegas?'

'No...' said Nicolai. 'Daddy married mummy in Moscow...'

'Right,' I said, as we hit the road. 'Who knows where we're going now? Come on! We're going to Los Angeles...'

Charlie, like many Americans, was under the impression that LA was not part of the United States. 'Well, we have been in America a long time,' he said sagely. 'So it's nice to be going somewhere different...'

I informed him that Los Angeles was in America and that we were going to see some friends who lived there. Then we were flying home to England — and to mummy. 'Does the pilot know we're coming?' asked Nicolai.

'Of course.'

'And does he know the way?'

'Yes,' replied Charlie. 'He's got a map...'

We left Vegas and reached California in an hour. There were now only three days before our flight home but, much as I was looking forward to seeing Charlie and Molly (and, soon afterwards, Khelga), I didn't want our trip to end. I coasted leisurely to our last KOA in Barstow and, next morning, tidied up and had the oil changed. (I was delaying our arrival in LA.)

But late that afternoon we hit a six-lane swirl of cars. This was our final destination — the city of tremors, toxic smog and traffic. All the cars hooted. Drivers gesticulated. I had to do seventy just to stop cars ramming me.

189

Within ninety minutes we arrived at a neat suburban street. Charlie and Molly ran out. 'Hi, you guys!' screamed Molly. 'Gee, how you boys have grown!' We entered the house. Charlie and Nicolai commandeered the toyroom.

We spent three nights with Charlie and Molly and I'm almost ashamed to say that we did little but talk. It was just fantastic to see them (and two-year-old Isabella for the first time – although she seemed shell-shocked at the boys' arrival). I wasn't in the mood for sights and my only obligation was to take a cover photo for this book.

I'd made endless earlier attempts (usually handing the camera to America or Julia – or setting the self-timer and placing it on a rock) but had never managed to capture the three essential factors of fluttering flag, smiling kids and not-too-fed-up-looking me. We drove to the Angeles National Forest with Charlie senior and rattled off a film to no avail. He was struck by the basic nature of our enterprise. 'If this was for a movie, we'd have a wind machine for that stupid flag. And loads of treats for the kids...'

After a few minutes both boys were bored. 'I want to go now.' said Charlie.

I began to get tetchy. With only three shots left we didn't have the picture. Then a gust of wind breathed life into the flag. But still the kids refused to co-operate. 'Oi!' shouted big Charlie. 'Listen you boys!' They looked at the camera. 'Pink Knickers!' They giggled. Charlie snapped. We had the picture.

Next, I emptied the sewer tank (I'd done a hundred miles with it sloshing around half-full – if you didn't return the motorhome with it empty, there was a 'dumping' charge). Nearby Follows Campground was teeming with life. I emptied the tank and we went to explore the action.

'It's the Californian state barbecue cook-off,' said a man, stuffing his face with ribs. 'Twenty-seven teams from all over the country have each got five cuts of meat to barbecue – chicken, beef brisket, beef tri-tip, pork shoulder, pork ribs... Their meat's judged for texture, taste and appearance.'

The Californians won. We didn't sample their efforts but some burgers went down well. Following the judging, there was a shoot-out. Some cowboys engaged in mock battle before showing their guns to my boys. 'You from England?' said one.' You want a souvenir?' And he gave me a bullet. 'Don't worry, it's blank.' But I binned it as we left. I didn't want customs finding it in my bag.

Next day we took America to the airport (she was flying back twenty-four hours before us). But first, we washed the RV in a high-clearance wash. I fed a machine with cash, and water and soap spewed out of a hose. It took fifty minutes to clean the filth off.

By the time I returned our faithful motorhome, we'd clocked up six thousand four hundred and ninety-eight miles – nine hundred and ninety-eight more than I'd paid for. An assistant calculated the extra mileage charge (deducting expenses for oil and the lights repair) then we accompanied America to the airport in a shuttle and returned to Molly and Charlie in a rental-car.

During the next twenty-four hours, the boys and I spoke to Khelga ten times. She couldn't wait to see us. We were all desperate to see her. We flew home next day and arrived on the morning of 20 August. My brother Dan met us at Heathrow and drove us home. Khelga was at work but there were flowers and three Cadbury's Flakes on the table. The house looked neater than it had for years. Charlie and Nicolai went to bed, only waking up at eight p.m.

It's now six months later. Khelga's had promotion and I'm thousands of pounds overdrawn. But even if this book only sells one copy, I won't regret this adventure. I did what I've always wanted to do – crossed America coast to coast – and got to know, a *little*, this fantastic country. More importantly, I got to know my children extraordinarily well.

People ask me if they missed their mother. The answer is, of course. But small children are selfish creatures and they'd been so absorbed during our trip that they'd had few opportunities to *notice* they were missing her. (Khelga, in contrast, found some of our time away extremely difficult – despite being very absorbed herself).

Charlie started school two weeks after our return. Nicolai started in September. We still talk about our trip frequently. The only worrying thing is that they constantly ask where we're going for our next big adventure.

PS Trooper Moore was a man of his word. The book I lent him arrived in Los Angeles the day before we flew home.

If you haven't read the book I lent Trooper Moore (*Matthew's Travels – 10 Years of Trips for the Travel Show*) you can obtain a signed copy for £6.99 (p&p free).

In addition, my new book, *Across Canada with the boys and a granny*, is out in Spring 2000.

Julia and America couldn't make this trip and Khelga wasn't keen on us travelling with an unknown au pair. My mum, the boys' only grandmother, didn't fancy it as she knows me too well. So we advertised for a granny. The deal was this: in return for air fares, food and (motorhome) accommodation the granny would lend a hand. Hundreds applied. Final choice was a retired Scottish headmistress. Find out about our adventures and how we got on in *Across Canada with the boys and a granny*. Signed copies £6.99 each (p&p free).

Write to MATC Publishing, PO Box 11507, London W14 9FX. (Cheques payable to MATC Publishing.)

You're also always welcome to offer me work: lectures/speeches, conferences, TV series, radio programmes, weddings, barmitzvahs (but not babysitting). Please write to the address above, or e-mail me at matcltd@aol.com

FINAL MESSAGE

Many readers have noticed that I publish these books myself. And many have written asking how you do it. In response, I've put together a course on how to publish your own books. It lasts one day and covers the main elements of publishing – editorial, design, production, sales, marketing and distribution. I talk about my experiences and pass on the lessons I've learnt. Industry representatives also give advice. The course is held in a Central London hotel on various dates of the year. Cost is around £75. Be warned that self-publishing is very time-consuming and not hugely profitable. But it is immensely satisfying.